# High Schools in Crisis

Some of Mountain View High School's former staff and students. From left, Ellen Hall, David White, Ian Burney, Richard Handley, Tom Edwards, and Serena Handley. (Photo credit: Jill Watkins)

# High Schools in Crisis
## What Every Parent Should Know

ELLEN HALL AND RICHARD HANDLEY

PRAEGER

Westport, Connecticut
London

**Library of Congress Cataloging-in-Publication Data**

Hall, Ellen.
   High schools in crisis : what every parent should know / Ellen Hall and Richard
Handley.
     p. cm.
   Includes bibliographical references and index.
   ISBN 0–275–98198–3 (alk. paper)
     1. Alternative schools—United States.  2. Education, Secondary—Parent participation—
United States.  I. Handley, Richard.  II. Title.
   LC46.4.H35  2004
   373.73—dc22     2003062433

British Library Cataloguing in Publication Data is available.

Library of Congress Catalog Card Number: 2003062433
ISBN: 0–275–98198–3

First published in 2004

Praeger Publishers, 88 Post Road West, Westport, CT 06881
An imprint of Greenwood Publishing Group, Inc.
www.praeger.com

Printed in the United States of America

The paper used in this book complies with the
Permanent Paper Standard issued by the National
Information Standards Organization (Z39.48–1984).

10 9 8 7 6 5 4 3 2 1

The stories in this book are based on actual events that took place at Mountain View High School, but the students' names have been changed to protect their privacy.

# Contents

# Preface

The high school years represent a formative passage in our children's lives. And yet we are witnessing the continual decline in the quality of education in our public high schools. Shrinking budgets, burned-out teachers, and indifferent students seem to be the norm, and there seems little hope for improvement.

In response to this crisis parents are taking it upon themselves to forge new paths in high school education. Charter schools, independent study programs, and home schooling are flourishing nationwide, with nearly a million children being home schooled according to United States Census Bureau figures and 685,000 students enrolled in 2,695 charter schools, according to The National Charter School Directory 2003, Center for Education Reform. An article on alternative education published in the *Los Angeles Times* by David Pierson, puts the number of home schoolers at two million, although this number has not yet been confirmed by education officials.

Our years as teachers and administrators of a small, private high school named Mountain View in Ojai, California, confirmed for us that alternative education has established a place for itself in the lexicon of American education. This book provides guidelines and suggestions for parents hoping to improve the educational experience for their children, either within the public school system or outside of it. It contains a wealth of information on how classrooms can be designed for optimum student involvement, how creative curriculums can elicit enthusiasm, and how learning disabilities can be handled without resorting to "special education." It also provides insights into the burgeoning issue of attention deficit disorder. As the stories in the book reveal, teenagers thrive in a school atmosphere of caring and respect. They drop their defensive shield and become engaged when they realize that their opinions count and that no one will criticize them for expressing themselves.

Our high school evolved out of the newly spawned home school movement of the 1970s. Like all organic things, it forged a life of its own, with spurts of growth, creativity, and adaptations stimulated by the particular group of students enrolled. We allowed the school's elective classes to reinvent themselves based upon the desires of the students. Environmental studies evolved into video production and drama. Anthropology was replaced by philosophy and computer science.

We listened to our students' suggestions and complaints. We encouraged them to engage in local politics and to advocate for their viewpoints in the local newspaper. We applauded them for expressing their creativity in the form of poetry, music, and dance performed at our weekly assemblies.

Many of our students transferred from the public school system and most of them went through a period of adjustment before embracing our way of doing things. They weren't used to being on a first-name basis with their teachers or having classes that were never larger than fifteen students. They were often shocked at how well the entire student body got along and engaged in activities in which everyone was included.

Some of our teachers had worked in the public school system prior to coming to Mountain View. They were thrilled with the prospect of creating their own curriculums and having the creative freedom to experiment with various teaching styles. We encouraged this experimentation and often met as a faculty to share our successes in using a particular approach. At Mountain View we recognized that happy teachers are the ticket to a successful school experience. An entire chapter of the book is devoted to identifying the characteristics of good teachers, namely the dual traits that are vital for success in working with teenagers—care and compassion.

An aspect of our school that appealed to parents was its affordability. We were able to charge modest tuition fees so that middle-class families could enroll their children. We accomplished this by keeping our overhead low and renting classroom space from a local church instead of being burdened by a large mortgage and maintenance costs.

Yes, we provided a viable alternative high school education for hundreds of teenagers, but it definitely was not freeform. Our school was run within very specific parameters that included strict attendance and disciplinary measures for violating school rules. Although our rules weren't many, they included the requirement to behave with kindness and respect toward fellow students and teachers.

We allowed our teachers a good deal of latitude in the way they taught their subjects, but we also adhered to the state guidelines for curriculum content and offered the required courses for college entrance. We succeeded in placing nearly all of our graduates in either four-year colleges and universities or two-year community colleges. Mountain View students have been admitted to the University of California at Los Angeles, Harvard University, Bennington College in Vermont, and many other reputable schools. Our graduates have also forged successful careers in such areas as auto mechanics, software design, construction, professional surfing, and acting.

Because the Ojai area is relatively small (population of thirty thousand), we constantly bump into our graduates and catch up on their current activities. We've been invited out to lunch by our former students. We've received phone calls from graduates traveling in Europe to ask about a certain village mentioned in a cultural geography class, descriptive e-mails from graduates in the Australian Outback, as well as dormitory missives from graduates now attending Harvard. Our student alumni maintain a place in our extended family of acquaintances.

Perhaps the biggest difference in the way we approached education at Mountain View compared to the public school system was our belief in the inherent intelligence of children. Children are compelled to learn and simply need a safe, supportive environment in which to do it. Instead of seeing our students as blank slates ready to be filled up with information, we considered each one of them a potential genius. Our job was to draw out their creative intelligence by engaging them in learning activities that were stimulating and enjoyable. Another goal was to spark the light of creativity within our students so that they would embrace the material being presented in class and assimilate it into their own way of thinking about the world. We weren't out to mold them but to guide them into a realization of their own true worth as intelligent individuals.

Much of the teaching that occurred at Mountain View was based upon real-world experience. Our teachers came from a variety of backgrounds, with teaching rarely being their only career. Although each teacher was required to have a degree in the subject he or she taught, many of them had spent years working in such areas as journalism, non-profit management, video production, and outdoor education.

And although we enjoyed cordial relations with the local public school administrators, and often compared notes with them on students passing between our respective schools, we were never plagued by institutional interference. We weren't burdened by bureaucratic paperwork or held accountable for standardized test scores. We were able to pass this freedom of operation on to our students, who recognized the unique qualities of our school and often commented on those qualities to their friends. This was undoubtedly our best form of student recruitment.

At Mountain View High School we were free to try anything and proceed with what really worked. We have written *High Schools in Crisis* to pass along our discoveries and offer guidelines and encouragement for helping teenagers have a safe, relevant, and enjoyable high school experience. We also hope that this book will provide reassurance that change is possible.

## CHAPTER ONE

# What Teenagers Are Telling Us

As parents we were shocked to learn that guns and knives were showing up on the local high school campus. We were having lunch with a teacher friend and her matter-of-fact way of sharing this information disturbed us. She spoke of it as if she were commenting on the change of weather. This occurred a few years before we began teaching high school and our only frame of reference was the school experience we'd had when fistfights were rare. Why on earth would kids be bringing weapons to school?

It was only after many years of experience and investigation that we began to understand the degree of rage today's teenagers feel and how the school system is failing them, not only academically but in just about every imaginable way. In order to begin to understand the dilemma of school violence we first have to examine the shortcomings of the current system and attempt to comprehend the message teens are sending us with their behavior.

## THE HIGH SCHOOL DILEMMA

Today's teens are making a statement and backing it up with their lives. The actions of teenagers, epitomized by every school-related killing, are sending a clear message. Can parents read this message? Are we even listening?

We react with horror and shock. We hope these incidents are isolated and will fade from memory like other insane behaviors that are inexplicable. But no, the killings continue, and repeat with frightening regularity. We no longer dismiss them as isolated incidents. The violence in our high schools has become a fact of life.

As former administrators of a successful alternative high school, we believe that the message is crystal clear. An increasing number of teenagers are angry with their schools. They are directing the violence toward the schools, not at the family or the shopping malls or their sports teams. Their anger is about school.

They are not angry because they hate algebra or don't want to study the U.S. Constitution. They are angry because they don't fit in. They are angry at not being recognized as valuable. They are angry because they have nothing to look forward to. They have no confidence; they have no place in the school environment and they often feel invisible.

The argument that we should just attend to academics in high school and let the social life of teens take place under parental supervision after school doesn't hold water if we want safe schools. Students described the teenager who did the shooting at Santana High School in southern California as being a "picked on" kid who was short, skinny, and whose ears stuck out. And the two students from Columbine killed their peers because they felt like outcasts. Paducah, Springfield, and Littleton—the stories are frighteningly similar.

Fear is nothing new to the high school campus. The use of fear as a means of control has traditionally been part of schooling. Fear of going to the office, fear of not knowing the answer, fear of not being accepted into one of the various cliques, and fear of being called a "nerd" all contribute to this climate of intimidation. But evidence is mounting that today's teenagers are more fearful than ever in our nation's high schools. A Kaiser Family Foundation and Nickelodeon survey called *Talking with Kids about Tough Issues*, published on CNN.com in March 2001, identified bullying and teasing as the biggest problem at school for teens. But not until recently have they been afraid for their very lives.

As well-intentioned as schools may be, and God knows most school administrators and teachers give their best, something is seriously wrong. The teenagers who lash out with violent acts are really only the most visible evidence of a vast and deep-seated dissatisfaction and rebellion brewing in our nation's school system.

## When Fear Takes Over

Children of all ages have an intense drive to learn; curiosity is their natural state. They come into the world open and trusting, eager to touch, taste, and explore their environment. One of our jobs as parents and teachers during our children's formative years is to channel this curiosity. But the child's inclination to learn is undeniable.

When children are afraid, they are no longer open to the wonders of the world. Their defenses go up; they pull in and protect themselves. They shut off the drive to learn and go into survival mode. The worst fear a teenager has is of being rejected by his or her peers. We exacerbate this fear when we put our teenagers in a large institutional setting where they don't feel they are among friends but are scrutinized for their looks and behavior. They begin to feel alienated and in the potentially violent cases are labeled as "outcasts" or "nerds." Likewise, if a teenager feels powerless, he or she gains tremendous power by rejecting, bullying, or "putting down" a more vulnerable student.

If we are to believe the reasons teenagers give for committing acts of violence, it is precisely this kind of shunning and bullying that has made them feel like outsiders and driven them to identify themselves as outlaws. If we wonder why the school doesn't do something, we should consider that in a large institutional setting, we can't expect a teacher with thirty-five to forty students to be aware of this kind of meanness when it occurs, much less correct it.

## Violence to Self

The most serious and often overlooked aspect of school violence is the fact that many of these frustrated young people kill themselves. They are so hopeless that they commit the ultimate violent act of despair. This is an incredibly serious indictment of the schools. According to a report from the U.S. surgeon general, published by the United States Department of Public Health Service since the early 1960s the reported suicide rate among 15- to 19-year-old males has increased 300 percent. Suicide is the third leading cause of death among those aged fifteen to twenty-four. The tragedy of so many young lives ended must be looked at deeply. We cannot look the other way.

Many of the students who are shooting other students at schools also kill themselves, as did the killers at Columbine High School. What terrible despair is motivating these acts of violence to self? Some of the risk factors for suicide are social isolation; feelings of worthlessness, sadness, extreme anxiety or panic; poor school performance; rejection; and failure.

At our small, private high school we were able to closely observe the behavior and interactions of teenagers and how they changed once the aspect of fear was removed from the school environment. One of the most revealing moments occurred when prospective students stepped into our office for their pre-enrollment interview. This provided us with a snapshot of their school experience up to that moment in time. Sometimes these snapshots were quite revealing:

When Randy came for his school interview Richard was impressed with his candor and intelligence. When asked if he'd ever been in trouble at school he replied that he had blown up a toilet with a cherry bomb and been expelled. He was so forthright and honest that it was hard for Richard to stick the troublemaker label on him. It made him wonder how such an obviously intelligent and articulate boy could have become so "bad."

It turned out that Randy also had very low self-esteem and a tendency to inflict injury on himself. On one occasion he severely burned himself with a hot piece of metal, leaving a very visible scar on his forearm. His mother told us that he'd never developed positive friendships at his previous schools, was failing several of his classes even though he scored high on intelligence tests, and was getting into serious trouble.

We admitted Randy to our school with the stipulation being that he maintain a "C" average. The intimate, informal atmosphere of the school allowed him to relax. The welcoming environment also allowed him to drop the image of the bad boy and gain acceptance for his positive attributes rather than through self-injury or vandalism. Randy began to develop a more positive social persona as a result of this acceptance.

His mother reported back to us after his first month at school that Randy was bringing friends home with him for the first time to hang out, drink sodas that she stocked in the refrigerator, and play billiards in their den. The friendships that Randy made at our school formed the basis of the new social group that he maintained long after graduation.

## SYMPTOMS OF INSTITUTIONAL FAILURE

The high school as an institution is letting teenagers down on many fronts. A brief look at the symptoms reveals the level of failure. In this section we will consider the dropout rate, the incidence of cutting classes, drug use, and the worst symptom of all: increased campus violence.

### The Dropout Rate

Mike graduated from a small middle school where he'd been very popular and knew just about every kid on campus. He was a favorite with the office secretaries and even ran errands for them. But by the second month of high school he was ready to drop out. School for Mike was largely a social affair and the much bigger campus and impersonal atmosphere of high school took the joy out of it for him. He couldn't plug into this huge place.

With some help from an understanding class counselor, Mike decided to stick with it and even competed on the school diving team during his senior year. Mike graduated from high school but some of his closest friends didn't make it.

One friend named Mark has his own construction company and recently bought his first house. He is doing well, he reads widely, and he is charming and bright. He left school at sixteen. He said he wasn't learning anything. He just couldn't stand it any longer.

Ron also dropped out of high school. He was bored and found the social atmosphere stifling. Ron is married to a gem of a partner. He is a licensed electrician, owns his home, and rents an industrial space that he and his wife use as a workshop for her artwork and his sideline surfboard business. They are a colorful and creative pair who have built a good life for themselves.

Why did these two intelligent and capable young men not succeed in high school? Why have approximately 3.4 million persons in the United States between the ages of sixteen and twenty-four become high school dropouts? It is not always because they couldn't cut the academic mustard at school. It is often because they didn't want to. As they tell it themselves, they "weren't learning anything." They were bored and uncomfortable. They hated wasting their days and wanted to get on with their lives. The reasons given for dropping out of school by the U.S. Department of Education, National Center for Education Statistics, *Subsequent Educational Attainment of High School Dropouts*, include:

- Didn't like school in general
- Were failing
- Didn't get along with teachers or students
- Didn't feel safe at school
- Got a job

## Cutting Class

Class cutting, or truancy, is so prevalent that daily absentee rates are as high as 30 percent in some cities. Skipping school is an indicator of a future filled with problems for most truants. When these students fall behind in their schoolwork, dropping out may be easier than catching up. Several studies have documented the correlation between drug use and truancy, and there is a direct link between truancy and daytime crime.

A commentary written by Maricopa County, California attorney Richard Romley titled "Truancy a Serious, Costly Problem" (1998), dealing with the factors contributing to juvenile delinquency, concluded that absenteeism is the most powerful predictor of delinquent behavior. Vandalism of cars, shoplifting, and graffiti are daytime crimes that are on the rise. When police in Van Nuys, California, conducted a three-week truancy sweep, shoplifting arrests fell 60 percent. The punitive response to teenagers not going to school is predictable—including arresting and fining students, and even fining and jailing parents. Some jurisdictions go as far as placing students in foster care if the truancy is excessive.

Is anyone asking why so many students are truants? If we ask students, they say they were "bored" in school and cite loss of interest in irrelevant courses. Parents often blame bullying as the reason their kids stay home, and school staff believe truancy is related to family problems and peer problems. Can we detect a circle of blame here?

The most common school-based reasons for class cutting are:

- Anxiety about bullying
- Worry about course-work deadlines
- Bad relationships with certain teachers
- Feeling that subjects are irrelevant
- Being suspended
- Having a low reading level

The choice is ours to continue to criminalize class cutting or to address the causes of truancy. A study titled *Combating Truancy in Our Schools: A Community Effort,* by educational researcher D. Rohrman, suggested some in-school solutions, including giving students frequent praise, increasing teacher interaction with the entire class, asking open-ended questions, minimizing verbal reprimands, and de-emphasizing competition in the classroom.

## Drug Use

Drug use among teenagers is another indicator of institutional failure. Although we cannot directly link teenage drug use to their dissatisfaction with school, we feel that young people whose lives are satisfying and fulfilling are not drawn into drug use. Teenage drug use is an indication of a variety of pressures from peers, family problems, and social conditions. As educators we have witnessed firsthand the amount of drug use correlated to students' dissatisfaction with their lives, high school being one of the major activities in their lives.

Although adult use of illicit drugs is decreasing nationwide, use by teenagers is increasing. The National Center for Chronic Disease Prevention and Health Promotion's *Youth Risk Behavior Surveillance System* annual survey of 13,600 high school students, stated that in 1991, 5.9 percent of students surveyed said they used cocaine. The ratio increased to 9.4 percent in 2002. According to the University of Michigan's *Monitoring the Future Study 2001*, citing data from in-school surveys of 8th, 10th, and 12th grade students, in 2000, 20 percent of eighth graders, 40 percent of tenth graders, and 49 percent of twelfth graders reported having used marijuana at least once in their lifetime. Marijuana use by twelfth graders declined from 34 percent in 1980 to 12 percent in 1992. Use then rose to 24 percent in 1997 and was 22 percent in 2001. Among eighth and tenth grade students, marijuana use more than doubled between 1991 and 2001.

In a 1999 study conducted by the Columbia University Center on Addiction and Substance Abuse titled *No Place to Hide: Substance Abuse in Mid-Size Cities and Rural America*, the use of amphetamine drugs by eighth graders was 104 percent more likely in rural areas than in urban areas. The rural teens were 50 percent likelier to use cocaine. While alarmingly high, the prevalence of drug use among today's young people has not reached the near epidemic levels of the late 1970s. But the number of young drug users is steadily increasing.

## Campus Violence

The most dramatic symptom of institutional failure is campus violence, which is prevalent and of great concern to students. According to the National Center for Education Statistics report titled *Violence in U.S. Public Schools: 2000 School Survey on Crime and Safety*, released October 22, 2003, approximately 1,466,000 violent incidents occurred in public schools in 2000. Out of these violent incidents in both public elementary and secondary schools, around 257,000 were reported to police.

Statistics on bullying at school vary widely. The National Institute of Child Health and Human Development study titled *Health*

*Behavior of School-Aged Children*, published in 2001 found that one out of every four kids will be abused by another youth. Researchers for the National Institute of Child Health and Human Development estimate that 1.6 million children in grades 6 though 10 are bullied at least once a week, as reported by Nels Ericson for a U.S. Justice Department fact sheet in June 2001. A study called "Bullying: Perceptions of Adolescent Victims in Midwestern U.S.A." conducted by J.H. Hoover found that, 76.8 percent of students said they had been bullied, while 43 percent feared harassment in the school bathroom. The NCVS report also stated that students who have experienced prior victimization are more likely to carry weapons to school. A survey of ten inner-city schools cited in the report found that 22 percent of students carried a gun outside of school and 6 percent reported carrying a gun to school in the early 1990s, and as we have witnessed, these acts are taking place not only in the inner city, but in suburbia and rural areas as well. Parents and teachers are often taken by surprise when violence occurs on their school campus. And high school administrators can be in denial about the rising tide of school violence:

The need for additional sports fields became a hot topic in our community. One of the problems identified at a meeting on the issue was the lack of soccer fields available for the growing Hispanic population. A Hispanic woman who'd volunteered to be a liaison between local school administrators and non-English-speaking families stated that Hispanic teens were getting in trouble, turning to violence, and dropping out of high school. She suggested that giving them more opportunities to play sports would improve the situation. After she spoke, the boys vice principal from the local high school stood up and categorically denied any such problems with Hispanic teens being involved in violent incidents and dropping out of school.

Richard was surprised at this because he'd heard of many incidents of interracial violence occurring both at the high school and in the adjacent neighborhood. The problem had become so severe that several incidents required the police to be summoned. A group of concerned citizens had even created a Youth Master Plan and formed a nonprofit group to address the issue of interracial violence.

After the meeting Richard reflected upon the vice principal's statements and concluded that there was a great deal of denial going on at the highest level of the local high school administration. To imply that the school was free of interracial violence was ridiculous.

## Solutions That Exacerbate the Problem

After the spate of high school shootings in the late 1990s the prevailing response to this crisis of school violence was an intervention plan that included the following procedures:

- Long-term suspensions
- Search and seizure, including use of metal detectors and searching of lockers and backpacks
- Staffing school security departments
- Prohibiting weapons
- Creative conflict resolution
- Reducing child abuse
- Improving public housing

Here's a likely scenario resulting from some of these policies:

Try to imagine yourself as a teenager arriving at school on your very first day to be met at the door by an armed security guard and then walking through a metal detector. The bell goes off in front of you and one of the students has to take off his belt because the buckle is too big and then he has to walk through again while all the other kids watch and laugh. At break you try to go to your locker, but the lockers are being searched, so the hallway is off-limits. When you come out of science class all backpacks are being inspected on a special table. Wouldn't you feel a little paranoid? Wouldn't it seem like you were in some kind of lockdown? Would you feel safe and relaxed about learning? How do these measures help students to not feel fearful, frustrated, marginalized, and humiliated?

Many schools have purchased metal detectors and placed armed guards in hallways, measures that Assistant Superintendent Chris Casey of Stamford, Connecticut, and other educators believe are ultimately futile. "It won't work to turn our schools into prisons," Casey says. "I believe if somebody wants to get something into a school they will." In the article titled "Educators Ponder Big Change: Smaller Schools" that was published about the benefits of downsizing schools, quoting Casey, CNN Washington correspondent Kathy Slobogin also wrote that "the machinery and patrols can't inoculate a school from a student so alienated and lost that he drops out . . . or comes to school with a gun."

Declaring war on the violence does not prevent violence; it is a re-action that creates a war zone at school. It is not natural for teenagers to be this angry. Do we just accept violence as inevitable and crack down on the schools? Will heavy policing work? Will we build more prisons for juveniles? Will we continue to send our kids to schools like this? Would you send your kids? The root causes of school violence need to be addressed.

## NOT MEETING THEIR NEEDS

What do your teenagers need at school? What are their compel-ling interests? They want to continue learning about the world but their focus has shifted. In elementary school they acquired the ba-sic skills. They hopefully can read, compute, and locate the infor-mation they need on any subject. By age thirteen they also have acquired basic physical and social skills like playing ball and form-ing friendships.

But as they move into the teenage years, they want to find some-thing to believe in and identify with. Teens want to distance them-selves from their parents to find out who they are and what they stand for. In order to do this they try out different ideas and different per-sonalities. How will they know unless they try them out? Parents should get ready for some outrageous ideas and costumes.

Teens want help at school to discover what they are going to do in their future as adults and how to prepare for that future. Will the classes they take in high school prepare them for college? What if they have no interest in higher education? Will they be able to have a good life without a college degree? What are their talents and what can they do with them?

Teens are also vitally interested in developing their social skills and they need help. But schools are organizing them into classrooms of thirty-five to forty students and telling them not to talk. Schools are not meeting the needs of the insecure and self-conscious teenager who wants to become a self-confident, socially adept adult. Many teens retreat into worlds of loneliness, isolation, and sometimes anger.

### The Idealism of Youth

Teenagers are the idealists of the world. What would we do with-out their passionate stands for righteous issues? But do schools respond to this aspect of their nature with soul-moving inspiration, or do they ignore or, worse, suppress it?

Most teens are looking for something to believe in. They are asking the big questions: Where did I come from? Why am I here? What does my country stand for? What are my parents' beliefs compared to mine? In this effort to identify themselves, they often join groups making social statements. Some find a religion to give themselves to or a political philosophy to try out. Parents and teachers should welcome this exploration. If the parents are Catholics, they may expect experimentation with Buddhism or maybe even atheism. One young bright friend of mine became a Marxist to try on a philosophy contrary to his politically conservative parents.

The hypocrisy of adults becomes all too obvious to teens when we don't live up to our stated ideals. Teenagers are very interested in facts such as George Washington having owned slaves. Teens may challenge our beliefs. This is natural for them and good for us. One of the joys of working with teenagers is that they never let you become complacent. When as parents and teachers we are being challenged, we should hold our ground, but not dismiss teenagers' ideas. When we respond to their ideas with, "That is so ridiculous I don't even want to hear about it," we alienate them. Ideas are fresh to their minds and need to be taken seriously. Here's an example of how the discovery process was awakened in one of our former students.

When Rick came into Ellen's American Literature class a month into the semester, he tried to be as invisible as possible. He wore a baseball cap and pulled it so far down over his face that she began to wonder if he was asleep. When Ellen called on him, his comments were brief but to the point. So he was following the class discussion. He was obviously putting in his time until he could get out of school.

It wasn't until they discussed an essay by Ralph Waldo Emerson called "Self Reliance" that he came to life. He asked insistently if Emerson was actually saying that we should consider our own inspirations as being as valuable as those of any great thinker. He also wanted to know if Emerson really believed that true geniuses were those who honored their own truths. When Ellen assured him that Emerson did indeed believe this, he was on fire with the idea, and he pushed his baseball cap off his forehead to discuss it at length.

A week later we got a call from his mother asking, "What do you think you're teaching at that school?" Rick was now relying on his own thoughts rather than his mother's advice. On campus Rick was much more engaged and animated, calling himself a "Transcendentalist."

## Social Development

Is it a coincidence that the most formative emotional and social events of our lives take place when the part of our brains governing emotional responses is maturing? Daniel Goleman in his 1995 book *Emotional Intelligence* points out that "while the sensory areas of the brain mature during early childhood and the limbic system by puberty, the frontal lobes—seat of emotional self control, understanding and artful response—continue to develop into late adolescence, until somewhere between sixteen and eighteen years of age" (p. 226). While children begin to learn appropriate emotional and social behavior and responses in preschool, we shouldn't abandon that kind of instruction later on when they need it most. Some of these behaviors include:

- How to be kind
- How to get along
- How to work in a group
- How to handle criticism
- How to channel aggression
- How to communicate needs
- How to be assertive
- How to compromise

Our high schools can enhance emotional and social development or they can severely impede it, depending upon the type of campus culture that prevails. Is your teenager's high school a place where students learn how to have a productive conversation with their peers? Or is it a place where a few bright and articulate students dominate most of the class discussions and everyone else is either silent or uninterested?

With a small group, guided class discussions can teach teens how to navigate a disagreement and how to respect the feelings as well as ideas of others. A teacher can lead students who have no confidence in their ideas to overcome their fear of exposure. The anxiety of not being perfect can be alleviated when they see that all of the participants have limitations, either in delivery or in content.

Back in 1995 when he wrote *Emotional Intelligence,* Daniel Goleman accurately predicted the advent of the current high school crisis. Goleman described what he called an emotional malaise among teens and presented compelling data taken from a national sample of American children, ages seven to sixteen, to illustrate a sweeping deficit in emotional competencies. The data indicated an alarming trend as more children chose withdrawal as a means to cope with emotional challenges. They also became more anxious and depressed, while coping with fears and worries of needing to be perfect and feeling unloved, nervous, sad, or depressed. Children exhibited attention and thinking problems and became more aggressive. Goleman pointed out that the many "wars" that have been declared on issues such as teen pregnancy, dropping out, drugs, and violence are ineffective and in some cases exacerbate the problems unless they include a component that teaches emotional competency.

So what is emotional competency and why is it so important? In short, emotional competency programs help teens identify and manage feelings and learn impulse control. Teens also learn to make better emotional decisions by first controlling the impulse to act and then identifying alternative actions and their consequences. Here's an example of how a student was gently encouraged to develop emotional competency:

Tina was an attractive but sullen girl who'd grown up quickly and had experimented with every kind of taboo activity before deciding to settle down and apply herself to school. Even though she'd made big changes in her life choices she still displayed an edge and had a habit of lashing out at teachers and fellow students when she felt that her sense of dignity had been violated. After a series of clashes with a young and wholesome first-year teacher we decided to bring Tina into a mediation session so she and the frustrated teacher could work out their differences. We arranged the session so that both Tina and the new teacher could state their points of view about their clashes.

The teacher said she was fed up with Tina's rude behavior, constant interruptions, and inappropriate comments when she thought the material the class was studying was dull. It came to light that Tina felt the teacher was taking her behavior all too seriously. She said she often came off as rude and indifferent when that was not her intention.

The process of letting Tina talk about her opinion of the class and her behavior, together with the teacher's feedback, helped her to see that she could indeed change the way she behaved in class. We suggested some alternative responses that she could use when she wanted to make comments. The mediation helped Tina see how her mode of expression was affecting other people and how she could improve the classroom atmosphere. The new teacher also developed a better sense of what motivated Tina's comments and was less reactive.

Goleman lamented the fact that there is little or nothing in the standard education of teachers that prepares them for this kind of teaching. He also stressed the need to raise the level of social and emotional competence in teenagers as part of their regular education.

Goleman also said that we must expect teachers and administrators to be reluctant to yield yet another part of the school day to topics that seem so unrelated to academic basics. But he pointed out that emotional literacy programs actually improve student academic achievement scores and school performance. He advocated building a campus culture that makes school a caring community, a place where students feel respected, cared about, and bonded to classmates, teachers, and the school itself.

## Sexual Development

We are not meeting teenagers' needs as sexually emerging young men and women. We teach them about biology but not about relationships. At the same time we are exposing them through the mass media to sexuality at an ever earlier age. Our young teens and pre-teens are becoming sexually active with very little to guide them. Once awakened, the sexual drive becomes compelling. But teens don't know what to do about their curiosity. Many are totally distracted at school by sexual issues. Sex is on their minds all day, throughout all of their classes.

Schools are preparing them for college and jobs, but the question of what to do about their sexuality from ages fifteen to twenty-five is not addressed. We look the other way. What are we telling them about these ten years as a single person? We are literally just throwing them into a world full of pitfalls and terrible potential tragedy without any guidelines.

We are not proposing that teenagers' sexual mores be determined, guided, or even addressed by the schools rather than the family. The issue is that their confusion about their sexuality is affecting their school day. For many teenagers, unresolved sexual issues are overriding everything else in their lives, including school. Even younger kids say they are feeling the pressure at school. The *Talking with Kids about Tough Issues* survey conducted by the Kaiser Family Foundation and Nickelodeon found that 49 percent of twelve- to fifteen-year-olds called the pressure to have sex "a big problem."

As a society we are giving kids some strange and contradictory messages about sexuality:

- Teens get a clear message from society to be sexually attractive but receive no clear messages about promiscuity or abstinence.
- Teenage girls are told it's a good idea to marry and have children in their mid-twenties but are also told to wait and establish their career before they have kids.
- Teens are told that just "falling in love" is not a good enough reason to marry, but getting married strictly for financial or social reasons is certainly not recommended either.

Schools do address some things to avoid (like having unprotected sex, with its risks of pregnancy and sexually transmitted diseases) but not how to create a life of loving and meaningful relationships. We do not teach about the development of intimacy, the hard work of maintaining loving relationships. Are we too cynical to teach that it is through giving joy and love to others that we find our own fulfillment?

This confusion is relatively new to humans. In ages past, when a young person was biologically ready to have children, the pairing or marriage took place and with it came the responsibilities for food, shelter, child care, and the like. We have created a time between childhood and adulthood when people are sexually active but not encouraged to have children. We send them off to war and give them credit cards and car keys, but tell them not to have sex until they are "adults." This society continually gives teenagers confusing messages about sexuality, parenthood, and "coming of age."

**Intellectual Development**

The teenage years are the years for the development of intellectual inquiry. In elementary school children don't question what they are taught, but high school students are interested in thinking about what they are learning. They are capable of making insights and developing ideals. They can make independent decisions and think things through.

What do we offer these fresh, capable minds? Are we providing anything for them to chew on or just continuing the rote memorization of elementary school? Educators have thirty years of studies at their disposal to confirm that learning takes place through active involvement that allows students to discuss, to create, and to engage in the learning process. And yet we perpetuate the lecture model in high school, where the teens are passive listeners. Overall we are not engaging them in the dialogue of learning.

A large percentage of high school graduates entering college have to take remedial English classes just to acquire basic writing skills. Scores on the National Assessment of Educational Progress show that while eight in ten students have mastered writing basics in grades 8 through 12, only a quarter are proficient. These findings were released at the Education Writer's Association's annual conference held in 2003. According to an article by Ellen R. Delisis titled "California Colleges, High Schools Collaborate," the California State University System allocated $9 million to an initiative to help freshmen improve their math and English skills. Almost one in three who enter college need remedial classes before he or she can handle basic freshmen courses. Nearly one in four seventeen-year-olds reads below grade level. We cannot even claim to be meeting the fundamental academic needs of high school students. And this is at a time when all the other needs of teenagers are being scrapped in an attempt to focus on academic achievement.

## THE ROLE OF EDUCATION

Why are teenagers in school in the first place? Obviously to learn what they need to know to be successful in their lives as adults. A standard academic curriculum has been designed to revolve around English, math, social studies, and science, with electives in the arts and physical education. This curriculum matches the intellectual abilities of most of the students, and some are excelling.

But from our previous discussion it is also obvious that this curriculum is not meeting all of the students' needs. We have witnessed the results of trying to isolate one aspect of teenagers—their minds—and place our educational focus in that direction. We are losing them, not all but far too many. The institutional atmosphere alienates teens at a time when they need mentoring. They need personal relationships with adults they admire and strong bonds with caring advisers.

We find movies about adults mentoring teens, such as *Finding Forester, Dead Poets Society, Good Will Hunting,* and *Mr. Holland's Opus,* very moving. These are movies about relationships. We know that teens want to be inspired and want to be friends with adults they admire. The theme of all these movies is the same. True learning is more than the passing of information from one mind to another.

As parents we know the importance of good teachers in the lives of our children. It is never more important than during the high school years, when our teens are expanding their social horizons outside of the family. Chapter 5 is devoted entirely to the importance of good teachers in the lives of teens.

## Exclusively Academic?

Although academics have traditionally been the focus of education in high school, academic success has been diminished for many students by devastating social, emotional, and sexual concerns. The classic definition of education is an experience that addresses the whole student: mind, body, and spirit. Adolescents' minds are affected by their maturing bodies and their spirits seeking inspiration. Teens are craving the richness and depth of the life experience, not the isolated information they can get from an encyclopedia.

Nurturing the "whole child" has traditionally been the job of parents. But our modern culture seems caught in a vicious cycle. U.S. Census Bureau statistics published in September 2001 show that parents have less time to spend at home, with 16.4 percent of all families now being guided by a single parent and 51 percent by two working parents. If the schools are also failing the children, then they have even less chance to develop into well-integrated adults, thereby perpetuating the cycle.

We can begin to reverse this cycle by realizing that school is where formative social interactions begin to take place. When we introduce emotional and social competency programs into our schools, the academics are bound to improve. Daniel Goleman cited several studies in *Emotional Intelligence* to show that social and emotional competency programs result in improved intellectual performance. One is the Yale–New Haven Social Competence Program conducted in New Haven public schools. Another is the Resolving Conflict Creatively Program conducted in New York City Schools in grades K–12. These studies showed improvement among students in problem-solving and communication skills when compared with a control group who didn't participate.

In many ways school is the incubator of our culture and we miss the opportunity to really have a positive impact on society if we ignore the social and emotional lives of students. It seems obvious that society would benefit from the creation of a campus culture of caring.

## Scaling Down to Enhance Learning

One of the ways to move toward accomplishing the task of transforming schools is to make them smaller. By shrinking the size of schools and moving away from the institutional atmosphere, we will have more opportunity to foster the kinds of caring relationships needed to truly educate the whole child:

Angie heard about our school through one of our former students and wanted to enroll even though she lived an hour's drive away. During her interview she said she felt alienated at her current school, with its vast number of students, chain link fences, and security guards.

During her first day in Richard's world history class Richard asked a question and Angie immediately raised her hand with a thoughtful answer. Richard praised her for her obvious knowledge of the subject and her face lit up. She then looked around at the other nine students in the class to assure herself that they all recognized her intelligence as well.

From that day forward the light never seemed to go out of Angie's face and she began to claim our school as her own. She later said she enjoyed the one-on-one contact she could have with her teachers. Even though her exuberance in class sometimes caused distractions, Angie was accepted by students and teachers and was recognized as an integral part of the school, even a leader.

During her senior year her mother told Richard that Angie had never considered attending college prior to enrolling in our school. Her experience with us had apparently demonstrated that learning could be fun and could make her feel good about herself. She also saw the benefit of having a college education, because the teachers at the school who were her friends all had college degrees. After high school graduation she was accepted into the University of California and completed a degree in anthropology.

## TWENTY QUESTIONS FOR PARENTS

1. How does your teenager feel about school?
2. Does your teenager complain about being bullied or left out?
3. Does your teenager express fear of going to school due to a problem with another student?
4. Is your teen afraid of violence or harassment at school?
5. Does your teenager dread facing a particular teacher?
6. Has your teenager ever talked about doing harm to him- or herself?
7. Does your teenager complain of boredom at school?
8. Does your teenager complain that he or she isn't learning anything?

9. Does your teenager feel that school is a waste of time?
10. Does your teenager want to drop out and get a job?
11. Has your teen been cutting classes?
12. Is your teen truant from school on a regular basis?
13. Is your teen failing classes?
14. Has your teen been suspended from school?
15. Are you aware of drug use by your teenager?
16. Are you supporting your teen's idealism?
17. Are your teenager's relationships with the opposite sex distracting him or her from school?
18. Are you crediting your teenager for his or her emerging intellectual ability by engaging him or her in adult discussions?
19. Does your teenager have an adult friend, mentor, or teacher whom he or she can and does talk with?
20. Does your teenager have a positive outlook for the future?

## CHAPTER TWO

# A New Model for the Classroom

The architecture of high schools across the nation imposes a negative framework for educating teenagers. The basic design of these buildings and how they are organized goes back to the 1950s, when there was a movement to consolidate small schools into large schools. The square buildings and classrooms opening onto long corridors were created to increase efficiency, especially for the administration.

U.S. Education Department data published by Kathleen Cushman show that between 1940 and 1990, the number of elementary and secondary public schools in the United States declined 69 percent from approximately 200,000 to 62,037, despite a 70 percent increase in the student population. The 117,108 school districts that existed in 1940 have experienced dramatic consolidation, decreasing by 87 percent, to 15,367 in 1990.

These behemoth schools are not serving us well. A complete restructuring of high school facilities is needed, as the current design pushes teenagers into an environment contrary to the way they learn. The first and most important change should be a reduction in the size of high schools. Research has shown that students have better attendance, are less likely to drop out, exhibit fewer discipline problems, and perform better when attending a smaller high school.

In this chapter we will look at a new and different model for classrooms, for school facilities, and for the location of facilities in the community. We will also address the reasons these changes are needed, from the perspectives of teachers and students.

## THE CLASSROOM

The classroom is the core of the school—it is where learning takes place. But parents rarely see what goes on inside the classroom during a typical school day. This section gives parents a glimpse into what their teenagers face and how the classroom can be improved.

After all the preparation for school—the bus ride, the homeroom initiation, locating the first-period class—finally the student is seated in his or her classroom and presumably ready to learn. In the old model the structure of this room gives the student many messages. He or she will be sitting in one spot for the next fifty minutes, part of a captive audience, placed in a row of others like cups in a cupboard, the message being that the student is indistinguishable from the many. The teacher is facing the student, and the teacher is standing. The message is that the teacher is the important person and the focus of attention. Additionally, the message is that the Many are to acquire the information from the One.

The rules are explicit: Do not to talk to the teacher or other students unless called upon, and stay attentive—no doodling, window staring, note passing, flirting, whispering, eating, or fidgeting. Do not question the value, importance, or reason for learning the material presented. Adults know best and the curriculum has been established by a board of education. The student is to be passively receptive, quiet in body and obedient in mind . . . until the bell rings, and then he or she can be loud and active for five to ten minutes before the next class begins.

Why do we continue with this model of the classroom when we have at least thirty years of research indicating that *active involvement* of students is what produces effective learning? Long before this, in the early part of the twentieth century, renowned educator Maria Montessori demonstrated that all learning begins with practical experience.

In the new model, when the traditional lecturer/listener design is replaced with a variety of dynamic forms, the result is active involvement. Picture a classroom where the following is taking place: The teacher presents a real problem for the students to consider and elicits their active response. Students break into small groups, research and answer a focused question by discussion and agreement, and then present it to the larger group. Presentations include role playing of a historical character by one group and drawing a diagram on the blackboard by another. Students will not fall asleep, doodle, or fidget, as they will be actively involved in learning in this classroom.

Involving students in discussions fosters retention of information much better than lectures do, and yet up to 90 percent of teachers use the traditional lecture as the primary instructional strategy. Learning involves not just the recall of facts but comprehension and evaluation of concepts, and so questioning and discussion are critical. Drawing out the student's thought is done by skillful questioning. By talking, students often discover what they think.

How can we change the structure of the classroom to facilitate this active learning? First of all, thirty to forty kids are too many for one or even two teachers to handle. Small groups of six to eight are best. But if you were to take a class of forty students and break them into small groups, all working in one large room, you would create a decibel level that would be intolerable. Can you imagine five groups of teenagers carrying on simultaneous conversations in the same classroom?

The ideal classroom is flexible, with no more than twelve to fifteen students. This size is supported by a preeminent twenty-year study conducted in Tennessee called STAR, or Student/Teacher Achievement Ratio. STAR concluded that the greater the class size beyond seventeen, the less likelihood that learning outcomes will be positive. Earlier research suggests that the most dramatic gains accrue when class size shrinks to fifteen or fewer students. In a classroom of this size, tables can be moved to accommodate discussions. When the results of the small groups are presented to the entire class, a circle of chairs works best.

In this model the "tourist students"—youngsters passing through without ever connecting—would be eliminated. Instead of sitting passively for fifty minutes, students move regularly to form groups, rehearse oral presentations, and join circles with others to listen to group presentations. Each of the students participates in the day's lesson with his or her peers. The students tackle a learning task, learn social skills, and actively participate.

Here's an example of a tourist student who transformed himself into an engaged and creative student.

Rob breezed onto campus for his first day of school in dark glasses, a tailored sports shirt, and an aura of coolness. He'd transferred in with decent grades and no behavior problems, but complained that the school he'd transferred from was boring him to tears. Rob kept up with his homework and seemed to enjoy our lively classroom atmosphere even though he didn't participate in discussions. We suspected that Rob's reluctance to participate was based on his notion that it was uncool.

Gradually Rob opened up to express his astute opinions about the literature being studied in his English class. One day he slipped a single sheet of paper across the teacher's desk. While the other students took their seats the teacher began to read a very well written, even inspiring poem. She asked Rob if she could read it to the class and he consented, while maintaining his coolness. The class was awed.

Thus began a steady stream of inspiring poems that were shared in class. During this period Rob moved out of his cool containment phase and became an integral member of the school culture. As a senior he won a poetry and art scholarship and continued his creative pursuits in college.

## Rows or Circles?

The placement of the furniture in a classroom is crucial. Active participation is achieved when chairs and tables are organized in a room so that students face each other and the teacher. A circle of chairs pulls the energy to the middle of a group, whereas rows focus the energy toward the front. Rows do not promote cooperation; they make a student either want to stand out from the rest or hide and sink into oblivion. Most often rows create passivity. In rows the students cannot actively relate to anyone except the teacher, and can only talk when called upon.

When students enter classrooms that are designed for active involvement, they behave differently. With furniture arranged for roundtable discussions, there is no back row in which to hide, nor are students able to sit in the front row and "kiss up" to the teacher. The subject at hand becomes the focus of the circle. Placing students in a circle changes the dynamic and facilitates discussions. Students do not look at each other's backs but meet each other's reactions to comments face to face.

In a circle, no point of view is given a greater or lesser importance; all points are equally accessible and equally regarded by the center, from which all originates. The circle is the shape of atoms, cells, seeds, and planets and a symbol of completeness and integrity. It affords total inclusion and acceptance with the attributes of simultaneous potential and fruition.

We found that ninth graders are almost universally unable to hold a discussion with their peers. They don't know when to enter the discussion. They either blurt out their thoughts, interrupting a classmate's train of thought, or remain silent as if watching a talk show on television. In our roundtable discussions we had to point out to the ninth graders how to listen, how to participate, how to recognize a thought worth sharing, how to help fellow students gather their thoughts and express them, how to stay with the subject, and so on.

Working to improve communication skills takes time from the curriculum, but certainly pays off with actively engaged students. The skills acquired from learning how to participate in discussions lead to years of successive and significant learning rather than to students who just put in time at school. Finding their voice is rewarding and empowering. When students came into our school they often mentioned that the level of class participation surprised them. They said that in the large institutionalized schools they had previously attended students did not talk because they didn't want to be laughed at or draw attention to themselves. Here is an example:

We met Tom's parents first because he wouldn't come with them to check out the school. His parents said he was very smart and creative, that he was engaged in learning all day. He designed computer software and was writing his own music as well as completing home school assignments. He didn't want to go to school, but the parents were looking for a small school where their shy son could socialize with other teens. They liked our family atmosphere.

When we met Tom he was not very forthcoming and even avoided eye contact. A small boy, polite but unexpressive, he looked around and decided he would at least try our school. Tom never missed a day of school and was an "A" student, but he balked at the prospect of an oral report due at the end of the semester in cultural geography. The project involved picking a country or culture, researching it, and writing an extensive paper describing specific aspects from the viewpoint of a tourist. This imaginary journey was to be shared with the class.

Tom came up to the teacher after class and said that he didn't do oral reports. She told him to just write the paper, after which they would address his discomfort. Tom was the last person to give his report. When called upon, he said, "Don't you remember, I can't give oral reports." The other students said, "We are with you Tom. We are just your friends, we'll help." He said, "I can't." The kids said, "Just read it, Tom, we'll be here for you." When he began, he tripped over some words and started to sit down, but they urged him on. One girl got up and stood next to him to provide support. Tom made it through the report triumphant! It was an outstanding and entertaining report and he was rewarded by applause.

By the end of the year, Tom was performing his own compositions on the guitar at an assembly in front of the entire school with confidence and the ability to share his considerable intellectual and musical gifts. He formed a musical group and made many friends at the school. The last time we saw Tom, he was performing his original music at a local outdoor concert as the lead singer and guitarist in a great-sounding band.

## The Classroom as Workshop

High school students need a classroom where the desks can be removed or rearranged to create a workshop space. Very little learning takes place passively. Rather, learning is stimulated when students move around, work with their hands, talk to each other, and discuss and create things. Much learning takes place when students work together, communicate an idea, produce a product, or accomplish a task.

At Mountain View High School we took every opportunity to teach lessons using a workshop format. This approach worked especially well for the natural science classes and in video production. Since we didn't have rooms specifically designed as workshops, we had to improvise. We used long institutional folding tables, which we moved around into any configuration desired and put back into the classroom format again before the next class used the room.

The earth science class studied every aspect of earth studies, from earthquakes and plate tectonics to ecology, botany, wildlife management, and the study of our local indigenous culture. We often broke the class into small working groups of two or three students and gave them assignments that they could work on together during the class period.

When we studied ecology these small groups used recycled cardboard boxes, Styrofoam, and other items salvaged from behind the local stationery store to create miniature cities of sustainable design. The students came up with all kinds of unique and creative ideas for mass transit, water recycling, and waste disposal. The ecology studies also required them to draw mountains, forests, and wildlife scenes on large sheets of butcher paper spread out on the floor and to figure out how building a road from the mountains through the forest might damage wildlife habitat and how the damage could be minimized.

The atmosphere in the classroom during these workshop sessions was active and lively. The students were noisy, talking together, and engaged in creativity. The only thing the teacher had to do was place time limits on their projects and decide when students would present their results to the rest of the class. It was during the times when we'd gotten rid of all the desks and were sprawled out on the floor working in small groups that the class atmosphere seemed most conducive to learning. The energy felt highly charged with activity. There was no boredom or idleness. Everyone was engaged, learning, and enjoying themselves.

Our video production class was even more conducive to the workshop configuration. We used the largest of our three classrooms as our movie soundstage, creating various sets for the movies the students produced. Part of the class period was spent learning about script writing and creating a viable story with character development and conflict resolution, and the remainder of the time was spent with the video equipment, practicing various shots and camera angles. When the time came to shoot the major scene for one of the student movies, we pulled the blinds down on all the windows to create the atmosphere of a discotheque, with flashing lights, tables with candles, and dancers. Students not taking the class crowded around the windows outside, trying to catch a glimpse of the exciting activity going on inside.

The exciting energy of creativity can be intoxicating for teens. But it takes careful planning, well-designed lesson plans, and clearly defined tasks and limits to effectively channel that creativity into productive results.

## Class Size Makes the Difference

Some of the obvious benefits of small class size are more personalized instruction and a more manageable classroom atmosphere. With a small class a teacher really gets to know the students. At Mountain View we not only knew all our students' names, but we knew their problems and their dreams. In an intimate setting, a teacher can see when he or she has lost a student's attention. The teacher can respond to a student's excitement for a topic or idea and extend the teaching to help a student who is stuck on a problem or a writing assignment.

Reduced class size is not the complete answer. But it does give teachers the opportunity for an expanded and flexible curriculum. It also provides an opportunity to help individual students. But can every teacher take advantage of a small class? We found that many seasoned teachers from traditional classroom structures were overwhelmed with the prospect of talkative, immature, hormonally charged kids and had no idea how to proceed with leading a discussion. Even with the reduced size, they resorted to lecture and crowd control. For some, the smaller size did not afford freedom but created new challenges.

High school teachers need to be introduced to the idea of drawing out and engaging their students without losing control of the class. It is a different model than the one currently followed in most schools. But in reality it is the essence of learning, and educational reforms that don't include this concept will not succeed.

Educators are finally recognizing the advantages of smaller classes. But most of the class-size reduction that is taking place in the United States is in grades K–3. At least twenty-one states, as well as the federal government, have launched class-size reduction (CSR) programs. For the 2000–2001 school year, the federal government allocated $1.3 billion to CSR in grades K–3, and the annual cost of the California CSR initiative was over $1.5 billion. Much of this effort is based on the convincing twenty-year STAR study from Tennessee, which found small class sizes in the first four years of school improve academic achievement. Students in this study were more likely to stay in school and go to college.

Due to the huge cost in restructuring, it may be a long time before class downsizing trickles up to the high school level. Fortunately, other innovations are being explored to reduce high school class size. It is possible. It can be done, has been done, and continues to be done. The small-school movement has created *schools within schools,* wherein one or more small schools develop within a larger "host" school. Then there is the *multiplex,* with one building specifically designed to house several small schools. Another option is the *scatterplex,* with two or more small schools that share a principal. *Charter schools,* publicly funded small schools run by parents and teachers, are also springing up across the nation. There are also *academies* that specialize in specific programs such as computer science or performing arts. At least fifteen hundred schools around the country are considering downsizing, according to Melinda Ulloa's report titled *Smaller Is Better, New Grants to Help Personalize America's High Schools.* The federal "Small Learning Communities" program to nurture this nascent movement awarded $42.3 million in grants to about three hundred school districts in 2001, according to U.S. Secretary of Education Richard W. Riley.

Concerned parents and private school educators are also collaborating to create and administer smaller schools. We successfully maintained our small high school campus in a rented church facility. Churches are ideally designed to serve as campuses for small schools. Church congregations often struggle financially and many only use their buildings on the weekends and evenings.

Our school did not intrude on the church sanctuary but rented the social hall/kitchen and three classrooms surrounded by parklike grounds. We were present only during weekdays, so the arrangement served both the school and the church. Our school had a maximum enrollment of thirty-six students spread across four grade levels. We found this size to be ideal.

### The Big Hall

In addition to small classrooms, every school needs a big hall. Our hall was large enough to accommodate the entire school, students and faculty. This was approximately forty-five people seated in a big circle, not in rows. The big hall serves many purposes, but it is indispensable in creating the community feeling necessary for a safe school.

Whenever our school faced a crisis, we came together in the hall. We also had weekly assemblies during which every member of our school community was invited to make announcements or share an experience. It was in the big hall that we built a sense of trust, where students came to realize that teachers could be vulnerable and students could be leaders.

The big hall served many other purposes as well. The room was carpeted and draped, but we removed the couches, as they gave an entirely wrong message to students. The music teacher could use the hall to ask students to get comfortable and listen to a piece of music with an ear to the structure of the composition. The big hall became the site of an Aztec maiden being sacrificed by the high priest for a cultural geography report. Yearbook layout, monthly birthday parties, video productions, and the showcasing of student films and live music occurred in the big hall. The civics class staged "Supreme Court" hearings on constitutional issues. The big hall was in constant use and experienced dramatic transformations.

Teenagers are eager to fill up whatever space they are given. They will sprawl on a chair or leap into a large empty room. The size and feel of the room play a role in defining their thinking. The big hall was a place where teens could break out of the confines of the conventional classroom and expand their creativity and expression. It also provided a space where all the students could participate in decisions affecting the school:

One year we had three candidates for prom queen from the graduating class. One of them was a colorful but somewhat overpowering extrovert who had been lobbying all semester to be the prom queen: Cynthia nominated herself. The other two candidates were more demure and had been nominated by classmates. Each was appreciated by the whole school for different qualities.

A discussion began in the big hall. If we voted for prom queen, would the other two be princesses? Was it even politically correct to have this competition? What was it based on—physical beauty, popularity? Were these good reasons to honor a student? What did it all mean? Many students, especially the boys, thought the whole thing was "pretty stupid." But others thought that it brought up issues of significance and should be examined. The consensus was: "If Cynthia wants it that much, we should give it to her."

After the heated discussion, the group fell into a few minutes of silent reflection. Cynthia jumped up and said, "I have and idea. Let's have three prom queens. We'll each wear the crown for one hour." For being such a good sport, Cynthia got to pick the hour in which she was to be honored by the crown. Our yearbook depicts the triad of prom queens in a state of much hilarity.

### The Great Outdoors

Teenagers want to be outdoors when the sun is shining and the classroom is warming up. It is far better to use the outdoors as the classroom instead of stifling this wish or trying to keep teenagers busy when all they want to do is stare out the window at the blue sky. A big advantage of having a small group of eight to twelve students in a class is that a teacher can easily arrange to take them out on the lawn in front of the classroom, down the street to a creek to study aquatic life, or in a van to the nearby hillside to study geology. Richard took every opportunity, especially in warm weather, to take his science students outside.

The advantages of outdoor activities for science are obvious. We were fortunate to have a national forest within a ten-minute drive of our campus and had easy access to native plants, rock formations, stream habitats, and earthquake faults. But even if your child's school is located in the inner city, a vacant lot affords opportunities for nature study.

Taking students outdoors doesn't have to be a major expedition. Sometimes Richard took his class outside for just a few minutes to view the types of clouds in the sky, to use a compass to locate the four directions, and to determine the direction the wind was blowing. And outdoor experiences are not limited to science classes. While teaching medieval history he took his class out on the lawn to carefully measure and stake out the size of a medieval home, including identifying a space for the fireplace and the sleeping areas. This gave the students a spatial appreciation of life during medieval times.

Richard also took advantage of the outdoors to allow his students to find a suitable place to pair off and work on assignments like creating a poster highlighting the amendments to the Bill of Rights or reading various articles on current affairs and creating a presentation for the class. These outdoor sessions, rather than distracting them, actually helped them to focus and discuss things out loud without disturbing the other groups. He simply made his rounds to the various teams, keeping them on track and offering suggestions if they seemed stuck.

Because we were located near amenities such as the city library, museum, and parks, we took advantage of these, using the park for all school sports activities and student entrepreneurial projects such as fundraising barbecues. The cultural geography teacher walked her classes to the used bookstore, five minutes from school, to purchase *National Geographic* back issues on their chosen research topics. We even had a natural science teacher who used one entire day per month to take her students hiking in the forest to study botany, biology, and stream ecology.

## A FACILITY DESIGNED FOR NURTURING

Richard's father was an elementary school principal and he visited his dad's school many times as a child. The most vivid memory of those years are about the occasions when his father's office was vandalized. Richard recalls looking through the doorway on one of those occasions to see papers strewn everywhere, chairs broken, and file cabinets tipped over. His impression was that some student had been very angry, not perhaps with his father personally, but angry at the mode of authority at the school. Indeed, institutionalized schooling can be dehumanizing—students rarely have contact with the principal except when they are in trouble. The principal's office and the entire administration building in the average public school do not present a welcome feeling.

## Administration Is the Heart

In order to alleviate potential alienation between the administration of the school and its students, the administration should be regarded as the heart and soul of the school and should be at the center of the school. This administrative center should provide the inspiration and direction of the school. Schools should be redesigned so that everything radiates out from this center. An administrative office placed at the center of the school can serve a vital function to students, staff, and parents. When we restrict access to the principal by shunting his or her office away from view, we create a sense of uncertainty and suspicion about the administration, which inevitably leads to fear.

Along with re-creating the school as a place of beauty, with grass, trees, and flowers, we should place the administration building in the center of a lawn or quad, and the building should have windows all around for full exposure from the inside and outside. The purpose of having the administration at the center of the school is to bring it back to its proper educational function and to eliminate the vast gulf that normally exists between the principal and the students. We want to make it more than a place where one is sent after getting into trouble. The administration of a school should be a very visible model of engaged and integrated leadership, with easy access to everyone involved in the school.

## Open Accessibility

Big windows for the administration office allow administrators to view the entire campus and watch the interaction of the students. The administrators are also constantly on display to the students. They can look into the windows and see an administrator working at his or her desk or perhaps smiling back at them. After a while the students forget about the concept of division between student and administrator and go about their business with a higher sense of security. Children are usually afraid of the things they don't understand. Fear is diminished when the unknown becomes known.

There are no secrets when the administration is placed at the heart of the school. This change reinforces the concept of the school as a community of learning, not a detention center with the principal as warden. The bullying and harassment that take place around school lockers are also eliminated when the traditional lockers with padlocks are transformed into the cubbies that we used in elementary school.

These cubbies are placed in the administration office, where they don't need to be locked and students come and go to retrieve their books between classes.

When students come to get their books from their cubbies they can hear what is said on the telephone by the principal and see what is on his or her desk. Students can come and go unless there is a conference or a private phone conversation. There is no such thing as an inner sanctum with access only to the "bad" boys and girls who get into trouble and are sent to the office.

Our school actually had three people who served equally in the administrative capacity, sharing some duties and also having specifically assigned tasks in addition to their teaching duties. The administrative desk was always staffed by one of these three people. They were available for student, teacher, or parent consultations, but no tasks took priority over the primary role of facilitating learning.

We think more than anything it was the visibility and easy access that made our system really work. The activities of the administration were fully visible and understandable to anyone who was curious about them. The role of leadership was being visibly demonstrated on a daily basis. In this way the administrator became the facilitator and the ambassador of the school rather than the enforcer of rules.

### No Fear

The only time Richard went to the principal's office as a high school student was when he got into trouble. He never dreamed of going near the place otherwise. Principals and particularly vice principals seemed like odious people who cast a spell of gloom and fear when they appeared.

When we place the administration building at the center, open it up, and spread out administrative tasks to a group or committee, there is no fear of the principal. Students enjoy coming into the office and can actually talk with an administrator, seek help with a problem, or ask a simple question. This system eliminates the Gestapo feeling in the office. There is no boys or girls vice principal whose main job is to administer punishment. The students are not afraid of this system. Teachers and students are free to come and go from the office to borrow supplies, use the copy machine, or use the phone to call home. The kids at our school actually demanded entrance when the door was locked. They had absolutely no fear of entering the office to go to their cubbies or to borrow something.

## No Bells or Buzzers

Anyone who has worked on an assembly line in a manufacturing plant will be able to affirm the effective use of buzzers and bells. There is a bell to begin work in the morning, a bell signaling the midmorning break, and the lunch bell. These bells continue throughout the day until the final bell and quitting time. Somewhere along the way this system of bells and buzzers was adopted by the public school system. Unless we are actually trying to train high school students for work on an assembly line, we should question the wisdom of continuing this practice.

Just think of the six years, starting in junior high school, when every hour, on the hour, kids have to rush to be in class on time or risk getting into trouble. What are we teaching with this antiquated system? It certainly doesn't teach punctuality as evidenced by the degree of tardiness at most schools. What these bells and buzzers do is to increase levels of anxiety and fear.

Another source of anxiety for teens is the early hour most schools begin, often before 7:30 in the morning. Research has shown that teenagers don't function well mentally at this early hour. They aren't as attentive or focused as an adult in the early morning. Starting the school day a little later, say at 9 A.M., and eliminating the irritating system of buzzers, could decrease tension and anxiety.

The first-period class at our high school commenced at 9 A.M. and there were no automatic buzzers signaling the start of each period. When we did summon the students to class, we rang a real bell three times, which gave them plenty of time to enter the class.

## Campus Architecture

The current block-building school design with rows of classrooms for two thousand students located along hallways with metal lockers on the walls is largely based on the factory model of the industrial revolution. While it may be an economical use of space, the noise in the hallways during class changes can be deafening, with students jostling each other, banging lockers, and crowding into the next class. We believe that the architecture of schools needs to be changed to reflect something different than the factory worker's view of life.

How many students have you heard admiring the architecture of their high school? High school buildings are often the ugliest in town, built to withstand the assaults of generations of teenagers imprisoned within them. Inside they walk the antiseptic-laden linoleum hallways to classrooms where cross-ventilation and air conditioning don't exist. Do we place a high value on our young people when we school them in structures with designs that are so oppressive? How can we expect teenagers to respect their schools?

According to the National Center for Education statistics, over half of all the crimes at high schools are associated with vandalism and theft. The largest age group arrested for vandalism is between thirteen and fourteen. Boredom, anger, revenge, and defiance reportedly cause vandalism.

Our school campus consisted of rented church buildings. This choice for a campus was due to convenience and availability. After a dozen years in the facility, we carefully analyzed the aspects of the site that enhanced the learning environment and those that detracted from it. We were fortunate that so much of what we stumbled upon was perfect for a small alternative high school. In many ways the space defined the school.

The buildings were in a beautiful parklike setting. The classrooms opened onto a covered walkway and then a tree-shaded lawn. Behind the classrooms was an enclosed yard with doors into each room. The office was at the end of the covered walkway, with easy viewing through a large window and an open door to the entire site. The parking lot was away from the buildings, a bus stop was on the corner, and a bike trail was half a block away.

The big hall and adjacent kitchen were set off from the classrooms, connected by walkways and surrounded by partially covered courtyards with benches and flowers. The campus had native oak trees and sycamores and views of the surrounding mountains, hence the name Mountain View High School.

In twelve years Mountain View was never vandalized, whereas the public high schools and junior high schools in the city suffered repeated assaults. Even the church that housed our school was broken into several times, but the school site itself was never touched.

Not surprisingly, we have discovered research that supports our theory about what constitutes appropriate school design. The School Design and Planning Laboratory at the University of Georgia is currently exploring how design patterns relate to student achievement. Most of the "essential design principles" from this study were met in our small facility. We see in this work at the University of Georgia and many other sources that the huge institutions of the past are being seriously challenged by a more learner-friendly school design. Here are some of the criteria incorporated in appropriate school design developed by C. Kenneth Tanner in a report titled *Essential Aspects of Designing a School*:

- Structures that reflect project-based learning
- Living views—gardens, mountains, and trees
- Outdoor rooms—partially enclosed space
- Centralized administration
- Small classrooms—accommodating only a dozen kids
- Covered walkways instead of crowded hallways
- Entrance in human scale, welcoming and defining

There were some things on our wish list, however: a hearth area, a physical education area, an outdoor stage. Because we believe that buildings in themselves teach, we would add several components if we were to design a new school. The list includes full-spectrum lighting, solar power, water-reuse design, and food-producing plantings.

## New School Construction

The future will see many new schools being built due to population growth combined with efforts to reduce average school size. In fact, nearly half of the schools in 2030 will have been founded since the year 2000. This brings up several questions about the future of educational architecture:

Will we design these new schools with the whole child in mind?

Will aesthetics be given more consideration than in the past fifty years?

Will schools be built in harmony with nature and with wise use of natural resources?

Will new designs provide for outdoor learning?

Will we see the end of trailer classrooms?

Will we build schools to the scale of small communities of students and teachers?

The design choice is up to us. Unfortunately there is a very polarized picture presenting itself for future school design. A reaction to school violence is creating a sense of urgency for school designers to more tightly control the movement of students and to even design media command posts for corralling news reporters in times of crisis.

On June 2, 2001, the *Los Angeles Times* published an article by Zanto A. Peabody titled "New Designs Turning Schools into Fortresses" that described how double-glazed security glass covered by metal grills and more sensitive alarm systems have become standard features in new and renovated schools in the Los Angeles Unified School District. According to the article, a new Burbank High School will be designed as one major structure with a primary entrance that will funnel students past a security guard and the principal's office. School designer Steve Wilkerson said such designs protect students from "crossing a sniper's line of sight during a rampage." A consultant to the Pasadena School District said that "schools should be built as securely as malls or banks."

But the article also quoted a number of juvenile justice scholars who questioned the need for some of the school security plans. Jason Ziedenberg, a researcher at the Justice Policy Institute in Washington, D.C., said that "when you start putting up fences and putting cameras around a school, it can cause undue restriction on the students and create a culture of control that does more harm than good." Some high school students quoted in the article also responded to the security measures by wondering whether the bars and locks installed to keep criminals out will make the school seem like a prison. "Are they locking them out or locking us in?" one of them asked.

Future choices regarding school design will depend largely upon what educators believe constitutes a safe school. Will students be protected by building fortresses to house them, or will educators strive to eliminate violence and alienation by making schools less institutionalized and more nurturing?

## THE SCHOOL AND THE COMMUNITY

With the advent of the smaller school it will no longer be necessary to find a large isolated space, preferably set apart from residential neighborhoods and downtown areas, in which to build a school. A school of fifty of fewer students can easily fit into existing buildings or share space with a church or community center. Bringing the school back into the heart of the community and perhaps even into residential areas will help students feel more at home and more connected with the heart of the community.

## Schools Located in Residential Areas

Our school was located on a quiet residential street just a few blocks from the downtown business district. Being so close to homes with the full spectrum of occupants, from elderly couples to single adults to families with young children, provided its challenges as well as opportunities for learning.

One of the few rules that we impressed on our students was the need to respect the people living in our neighborhood, to respect their privacy, their desire not to be disturbed by loud noise, littering, or loitering on their lawns. Our motives in this effort were twofold. First, we wanted to ensure that we maintained good relations with the neighbors, and second, we wanted to provide an opportunity for our students to learn respect and to feel more integrated with the community, not set apart so that they couldn't create a "nuisance."

Our location in a residential neighborhood worked very well and gave the school a homey and nurturing feeling. On the quiet street with its majestic trees, lawns, and tastefully maintained houses, the students and staff enjoyed an atmosphere of beauty that was reflected by the school grounds and radiated out into the surrounding neighborhood. Being in a neighborhood also reinforced an atmosphere of familiarity. The students were not subjected to an institutional setting that might contribute to feelings of alienation. On their way down to the neighborhood convenience store for a snack, they passed houses similar to their own with people out watering their lawns, working in their gardens, or taking their own children to school.

There is really no reason why the high school facility can't be at the heart of the community. We should be encouraging our students to feel at home and relaxed while surrounded by friendly neighbors, not set apart and surrounded by tall fencing that contributes to a feeling of being held captive by the school system.

## Bringing Experience into the School

It is certain that no matter how well informed teachers are, they are not the definitive experts on the subjects they teach. Adding the dimension of outside experts and people with experience in a particular field greatly enhances a student's ability to understand and see the subject form various points of view. We were always on the lookout for people who were willing to drop in on our various classes and share their particular area of expertise.

In Richard's earth science classes, while doing a segment on volcanoes, he was able to recruit a *National Geographic* filmmaker, who talked about his experiences and showed a film he'd made about the history of Oregon's Crater Lake. During a unit on energy Richard brought in a solar contractor to do demonstrations on how photovoltaic cells produce electricity from the sun. He also contacted a botanist with vast knowledge of local native plants and had him lead a field trip on native plant identification.

In civics class Richard asked a lawyer to speak on law and society. The unit on law enforcement was enhanced with a visit by a local police officer who had also worked for the Drug Enforcement Agency in South America; he shared some harrowing stories of his experiences combating drug trafficking in Peru. When Richard studied economics the class invited several businesspeople to talk about the role of the entrepreneur in the marketplace.

In the U.S. history class, while studying the McCarthy era, the teacher asked a woman to share her experiences after her husband was blacklisted as a screenwriter in the early 1950s. Perhaps the most memorable speaker invited to address the class was a ninety-five-year-old World War I veteran named Frank Noyes. Frank had served as a baker with General Pershing's expeditionary forces in France, and he arrived at the classroom wearing his original army uniform. He quickly won over the students with a lighthearted and somewhat irreverent account of his exploits in the war. This man, who was virtually a living testimony to a significant era in American history, made that history live again for the students.

Other teachers at the school also took full advantage of using the community as an educational resource. An English teacher brought in a poet who taught a lesson on Japanese haiku, as well as a local Shakespeare troupe to dramatize a play. The journalism class was visited by a photographer who showed them how to shoot pictures to accompany their stories. In the life skills class a banker was invited to demonstrate how to open an account and avoid the common pitfalls of credit card use.

All of these people were brought into the school from the local community. They forged intergenerational connections with the students and were honored to be asked to participate. Bringing the community into the schools will strengthen the bonds teens feel with that community.

## The Community as a Classroom

A vast store of information is also available outside the walls of the classroom, and teachers should endeavor as much as possible to tap it. The community at large offers knowledge and learning that enhance any curriculum.

Because our school was a quick five-minute walk into the downtown area, it was easy to take students on walking field trips to the library, museum, and local park. The benefit of having access to a large library is obvious, and we often took students there to introduce them to the librarians and teach the techniques of conducting research. We even allowed small groups to select books to read in the quiet library atmosphere.

The museum's educational displays on local history were ideally geared for students to use as a resource to answer study questions. The history teacher also found it useful when studying local history to take his students into the business district, where he organized a scavenger hunt requiring them to obtain as much information about the local history of our town as they could in one hour. On occasion the art teacher took small groups of students from her ceramics class to visit professional artists so they could observe a working studio.

The local park also served a vital function for the school. Each year we organized several all-school coed baseball games and the park was a perfect place to hold them. The park also provided space for the students to complete their unit on developing entrepreneurial skills. They sold tickets to the events they organized at the park, held a raffle, and divided the proceeds among the class.

If we are preparing our teenagers to enter the adult world, is it wise to keep them locked up in school until they graduate? Shouldn't we be introducing them to the lifelong learning available to them locally? Shouldn't they be exposed to the rich experiences and abilities of local people and educational resources such as libraries and museums and the wonders of the natural world around them?

## TWENTY QUESTIONS FOR PARENTS

1. Do you know if your teenager is actively involved in learning in the classroom?
2. Are the majority of your teenager's classes taught in the lecture model of straight rows facing the blackboard?
3. Do you know how many students are in your teenager's classes?

4. Does your teenager participate in roundtable class discussions about topics or merely provide right answers?

5. How do you rate your teenager's discussion skills at social events with family and friends?

6. Are you aware of any assigned projects in the classroom that your teenager has taken part in?

7. Do you consider the size of the high school in your community to be appropriate?

8. Has your school district considered any of the popular downsizing options such as schools within schools or charter schools?

9. Can the entire student body and staff of your teen's school meet in one room and face each other?

10. Does your teenager's school integrate the outdoors into the curriculum?

11. Is the principal of your high school approachable and visible every day for teens and parents?

12. Are the school offices in a central location with a welcoming atmosphere?

13. What is the sound level from bells, buzzers, banging metal lockers, and public announcement systems?

14. Is the high school the ugliest public building in your town?

15. Is the local high school regularly vandalized?

16. How can you contribute to the beautification, downsizing, and participatory classroom design in your teen's school?

17. Do you believe that we will be successful in creating safe schools if we design them more like prisons?

18. Is your school district planning for a new high school in the future, and would you be willing to request a modified design to reflect the concerns in this chapter?

19. Could you or someone you know contribute to the lives of teenagers by visiting a classroom and sharing expertise?

20. Could your business or club offer a destination for a field trip for a high school class?

## CHAPTER THREE

# The Genius of Every Child

The child is central to any discussion about restructuring schools. Without the proper attitude toward our students, we will fail to provide safe and effective schools no matter what reforms we initiate. Our experience has been that each child has a unique gift, a genius within. We are not talking about the "Einstein" model of genius but the classical definition that recognizes genius as the "attendant spirit," or one's natural inclination. When we learn to acknowledge the genius of the child, nurture it, and draw it out, we will be on the road to safe schooling. We need to recognize that every child's genius is worth nurturing. There is no such thing as a lost cause:

Pete was a big kid with red hair, freckles, large squat hands, and a lower lip that was often turned down in a pout. He avoided eye contact and his face was expressionless. He wore black T-shirts with dragons and skulls and had several earrings. In our first writing exercise he wrote of killings and possessions in gruesome detail. He responded to every comment about his writing as if he had been personally attacked. He defended himself from the dreaded teacher at every turn.

If we had responded to the personality mask Pete displayed, it would have been with revulsion, which, by the way, was exactly the purpose of the mask. Although most of the staff made an effort to look beyond the mask, some of us were convinced that Pete was not appropriate for our gentle little school. The mask was securely on and left little room for any light to penetrate beyond the surface.

The "breakthrough" came early in the semester during our all-campus beach camping trip. Pete showed us he could do amazing things with a knife when he whittled a replacement part for some camping gear and sullenly presented it to the staff. We expressed our appreciation and praised his talent. He lit up! He then took over chopping the firewood and throughout the trip continued to display considerable skill in camp craft.

Eventually Pete became the school's fix-everything person. He could get the VCR working when no one else could. He got cars running when they died in the parking lot. In pottery class he was amazingly adept at throwing pots on the wheel.

School was a bumpy road with Pete. We even had to ask him to stay home one week and really consider if he wanted to stay at our school. He tested our love but he very much wanted to stay. Pete eventually became a most affectionate and serving friend to the entire school. He was always there with a big bear hug when one of the girls needed comforting. He was helpful to teachers and was a loved, respected, and popular friend to the guys.

Pete never achieved great academic success. His way of thinking was a meandering train of thought that often took the class way off the track. His brain made unique connections. The best way Ellen can describe it is that Pete circled around a subject rather than taking it one logical step at a time. This was distracting, but we all listened and attempted to follow his thoughts. As we did this it became more evident that our acceptance enabled him to sort out his own thinking. Eventually we could work through an abstract idea with him and stay on the point.

Where Pete shined was in math, which he approached with the same kind of intuition and offhandedness that he used on an automobile engine. It was obvious to him how it worked and he automatically knew how to solve the problem as soon as he looked at it. Another subject Pete loved was the environmental studies video project. He enjoyed the group discussions, family atmosphere, taking care of technical problems, working the video camera as if it were an extension of his arm, and driving everybody around for the filming.

According to Pete there were several reasons for the mask he wore when he first arrived. He thought he was "too dumb" to be any good, so he just took on the "bad" look. Teachers had always humiliated him for his answers and his grades were deplorable. At a very young age he decided it was safer to shut up and just tune out. He insisted that he had never learned anything until he came to our school. We discovered that he needed glasses to see the blackboard and that his learning style was very different from the standard. His English term paper read like an instruction manual, but he did follow the directions in his own unique way. I suspect it was the first term paper he had ever completed.

By looking beyond Pete's mask, we witnessed his truly loving, warm, helpful self emerge. Gradually he lost the unapproachable look. He began to wear his glasses, dropped the extra weight, had his hair styled, and changed his dress to fit his new way of being. As his mask disappeared, a handsome, confident, and respected friend to all appeared underneath. He also discovered his own kind of intelligence, which was mechanical. Pete didn't go on to an "Ivy League" college, but we were all delighted when he chose to study automotive technology.

What if we had said, "You are that black T-shirt with skulls and earrings. We don't allow that look at our school. Either change or leave. You are a disaster waiting to happen"? We would have been responding to the mask and would have missed all of the beauty that was underneath. Also and most importantly, one wonders if Pete would have discovered his own Light.

We don't often hear teachers talk about drawing out the genius of their students. Most of their days revolve around the "teacher supplies the information, students listen and supply correct answers" format. The typical day of instruction consists of inculcating students with enough history, science facts, and writing skills to raise those standardized test scores. Correcting massive amounts of homework, dealing with endless announcements and paperwork from the principal's office, and maintaining crowd control also eat up a great deal of time. Recognizing uniqueness and individual creativity isn't placed high on the list of priorities, largely because of the time crunch.

## EACH HUMAN BEING IS AN EMERGING SOUL

Even though we regard the high school years as a time of transition, with greater responsibilities and accountability, high school students still need the same care and nurturing as younger students. Teenagers are emerging from childhood and are glimpsing their approaching adulthood. Teenagers often exhibit a tough exterior because they are so unsure of themselves. When making the shift from middle school to high school they quickly learn how to put up this tough image in order to survive. Dodging school bullies and learning how to parry the heavy-handed tactics of battle-weary teachers make them not want to develop their individual expression but become invisible behind an inscrutable mask.

It is only when we sit down with teens and attempt to connect with the people behind the masks that we discover their true identities. Teenagers tend to relax when we drop the condescending attitude and stop treating them as our charges who will benefit from our superior store of knowledge. When we treat our students as intelligent and capable human beings, then we begin to draw out their unique genius.

The trick is to look beyond the particular affectations of their age and see teenagers as souls experiencing one of life's passages. It helps if we admit that we are still being challenged by life's passages ourselves and therefore have compassion for their difficulties. We can make an effort to see the potential within them that they may not have seen or valued yet themselves. As we recognize their potential, we draw out unexplored attributes. They can discover themselves through our eyes.

### Discovering Themselves

The approach to education that we used in our high school was to draw out the natural inclinations of children by engaging them in discussion and activities in which they could express their individuality. High school students don't really know themselves very well. They need a variety of experiences and subject matters to explore. By arranging experiential learning opportunities that allow students to explore what they are good at, we can help draw out their undiscovered interests and inclinations.

In the traditional school setting it is not about students knowing themselves but about students knowing the material. Our approach of drawing out the student presented quite a contrast to the approach that the student is to be filled up with a standardized block of information. The winners in this system attend universities, make the money, and do well. The losers don't go on to higher education, work in service industries, and have a marginal life.

Our experience is that a successful life physically, mentally, and spiritually requires a process of self-discovery that begins in the teen years. The process of self-discovery is not accomplished by putting students into a competitive environment where they are pressured to assimilate the most information. It is about providing ample opportunities for them to look inside and discover themselves. The two methods described below illustrate how to connect with the emerging soul of teenagers at school.

1. *Draw them out on the first day.* On that crucial first day of school, we gathered all our students together in a large circle and asked each one of them to introduce themselves and tell everyone what they wanted to accomplish during the year. Their goals didn't have to be about academic achievement, and often students said things like, "I want to learn how to get along better," or "I want to get my driver's license." We wrote these goals on large sheets of paper and kept them until the end of the year to allow the students another look at them.

This fairly lengthy process made each student the center of attention as we recognized them as individuals with hopes and aspirations.
Their answers the first year were often not too stellar, since they may
not even have thought of the question before. But being put on the
spot got them thinking fast about what they wanted to do that year.

Another process we used was a game in which all the students and
teachers stood against the wall of our assembly hall. We asked all the
vegetarians to go to the opposite wall, while the meat eaters were to
stay where they were. We then used this process of walking across the
room to the opposite wall to identify the kinds of music they liked,
their travel experience, their favorite sports, movies, and actors, and
so on. This helped all of us to become acquainted with each other in
a nonthreatening way. As the groups we belonged to changed with
each category, we saw that we had things in common with everyone.
Right away this game provided students with a framework for themselves; they were not just unmemorable faces in the crowd.

We then had the students think about the four-year high school
experience and gave them the task of figuring out what classes they
needed to take just to graduate or to go on to college. They were given
a form and the teachers moved around the room helping with questions. The older students were adept at this and just made some al-
terations from the previous year. The first-year students were a little
baffled and challenged by this process. They were accustomed to being given a schedule on the first day of school and just finding the
right classroom before the bell rang. We were asking them to plan their
classes for the next four years. It was a healthy challenge and even if
they were not successful at planning that first day, the responsibility
was shifted to them.

In this exercise, we were drawing out their participation in, and
ownership of, their education. They had to take responsibility for gathering enough units to graduate. They had to know why they were
taking their classes. Few students came to us in the middle of the semester and said, "I want to drop algebra," because they understood
that they needed the class to get into college. Their choice to drop a
class had serious consequences and we were relieved of saying, "You
*have to* take algebra."

2. *Gear classrooms toward discussion.* We encouraged discussion
from the very first day of school, from the way the desks were arranged
in a circle to the type of assignments that were given. The teacher de-

fined the topic of discussion and required that the students be prepared with adequate research and information to construct an opinion or at least formulate some pertinent questions. But the teacher's
role beyond that was simply as a contributor to the discussion and not
as the authority on the subject.

With literature, once a selection had been read and comprehended
by the small class, an assignment was given that would elicit each
student's personal response to the ideas in the selection, as in this
example:

In the world literature class, the students read a selection from *The Prince*,
by Machiavelli. For the written assignment, Ellen asked the students to consider whether, if they were to choose a career in politics, they would use some
or all of the guidelines Machiavelli put forth for maintaining political power.

With this written assignment in hand, the selection was discussed. By talking about the assignment, the students could see that each of them had a
different perspective on the selection. As expected, some students thought
politicians would have to be ruthless or deceptive to get anything accomplished. Others thought Machiavelli's tactics were immoral. Often the students would ask for Ellen's opinion, which she gave, but not as the definitive
answer. Students were graded on how well they formulated and supported
their position, not on getting the right answer.

When the discussion was carefully moderated, each student contributed,
not just the talkative ones. These discussions created a culture in which students wanted to be thinkers. It also helped them to define their values, reflect on their beliefs, and find the truth within themselves.

## Acknowledging Their Contribution

Students need the positive reflection of an adult. When we establish an open and friendly relationship with our students, we can acknowledge their ideas and contributions and reflect back to them the
message that they are worth something and their ideas are valuable.
This recognition makes the student feel good and enables him or her
to express the genius that is within. We all need someone to reflect
back to us who we are, but teenagers especially need this because they
are just making the discovery themselves.

It has been our experience that when students feel acknowledged
and have a positive, open, and trusting relationship with a teacher, they
are more likely to develop confidence in their abilities. Through the
class discussion model we acknowledged each student's effort. We

always tried to affirm their points of view so they could build confidence in their own thoughts.

When a student has an interesting thought and manages to express it in front of his or her peers, a teacher can encourage thinking by restating the thought and complimenting the thinker. Encouraging discussion rather than right answers helps a student to develop his or her abilities to reason and to think critically.

Praise has often been touted as a way to encourage students. It is considered the carrot that makes the stick less necessary. But praise needs to be refined and carefully delivered to achieve positive results. We should not praise a student because he or she is smart, but because he or she came up with a well-thought-out solution: "You took the problem from point A through to B and on to a solution." Praise like this explains to the student what he or she has just accomplished so that he or she can repeat it.

Praise can create serious problems for high school students. Too much of it may get them thinking they have made the grade and reached the highest plateau with their efforts, or they may think they have the teacher hoodwinked. Just giving students strokes does not result in drawing out intelligence. Just because everyone feels good does not mean they are learning something. Praise is most effective when it is given in response to a sincere and successful effort and the student is told clearly what was admirable about what he or she did. Just to say "good job" is not enough. Why is it a good job?

**Giving Them a Voice**

Teenagers can be given a voice in the decision-making process of the school, especially in areas requiring creative thinking. This validates their opinions and helps them feel more confident about expressing themselves. It can be accomplished in the following ways:

1. *Let students have a voice in what elective classes are offered at the school.* We found it very helpful to survey our students on a regular basis about their interests. If a number of students expressed a desire to learn art history, we would arrange to offer that class. Our school had the flexibility to hire specialists in various disciplines so that introducing a new class such as yoga or theater production was easy to do. We also gave students flexibility within the classes themselves. In our music classes we allowed students to pursue the type of music they

liked best. The teacher allowed them to form small combos so they could concentrate on their particular interest rather than having them all participate in one large group.

2. *Allow students to have input when choosing extracurricular activities.* We took our students on two camping trips each year. These trips offered them a multitude of positive experiences. Their voice in the decision-making process also empowered them and engaged them in the activity. Instead of just being passive participants, they felt like their ability to make good choices was being acknowledged. Student choices included beach camping, ocean boat trips to an island national park, river rafting, alpine mountain hiking, and camping.

No one ever complained about being bored on these trips. There was full engagement because they had been part of the decision-making process. We also allowed the students to create the meal menu for the trips, do the shopping, and have specific assigned tasks once we arrived at our destination. This all added to their ownership of the activity and made it a truly community adventure.

### Creative Autonomy

Group projects come alive when teachers hand over some authority to the students and allow them to express creative originality. Simply giving them authority over the project acknowledges their capability to handle it. The purpose of the finished product is to demonstrate learning and not necessarily to be used as a showcase:

The history teacher was having a hard time motivating his world history class. They were a diverse and creative group who all seemed very tuned into music. They were constantly sneaking in CD players and listening to their favorite discs during the course of the class.

He finally decided to stop fighting this mass movement and invented a project in which the entire class would create a video that examined the history of music, from its origins up through classical, baroque, jazz, blues, and contemporary. The students formed small groups that were each assigned to research the era of music they liked best. The teacher expected all of them to choose contemporary, but that didn't happen and they took on the project with relish and enthusiasm.

With research in hand, the groups organized themselves into camera operators, sound technicians, script prompters, and on-camera narrators. As the project progressed the students branched out into the community and located musicians and musical historians who were willing to be interviewed about their particular musical expertise. The teacher's job was to provide the transportation and keep the project on track while they set up the interviews and arranged the camera angles, the sound recording, and the narration.

This history-of-music project provided them with a safe atmosphere in which to try out their ideas and learn history through a very stimulating medium. The classroom became a learning laboratory and it fostered a very experimental and exciting atmosphere. Although the music video wasn't meant to be taken on the road or shown on MTV as a glossy product, it did provide lessons in history, video technology, oral communication, planning, writing, and making contacts among adults in the community. It also provided an opportunity for fun, spontaneity, and experimentation. Everyone got turned on to the process of historical research and all contributions were acknowledged.

Let us contrast this innovation to what might happen in a traditional classroom for a teacher facing the same challenge. He or she would be required to cover a proscribed world history curriculum and would not be allowed to deviate due to testing requirements. The class, which would comprise over thirty students, many of whom would not be interested in the subject and would be repeatedly sneaking their CD-player earplugs into their ears, would have to be controlled. The teacher would have to interrupt his or her teaching to reprimand students, send them to the office, fill out detention papers, or do whatever school policy dictated. Or he or she could overlook it and just teach to the students who were engaged and let the troublemakers waste their time until the bell set them free. Would any of this teacher's students learn more history than the students studying the history of music through a video production process? In addition to world history, what would the students in each case learn?

## NURTURING RIGHT HUMAN RELATIONS

All parents, teachers, and students associated with the local high school are neighbors in their community and have a relationship that reaches beyond the school campus. While striving to eliminate alienation and nurture positive relationships at school, it is important to acknowledge this and to recognize students as unique individuals with lives outside of school.

Teachers and administrators should attempt to get acquainted with their students and take an interest in their interests. A sense of community can be created when schools get to know students' families and the things they enjoy doing on the weekends. Teachers and administrators can make an effort to relate to their students as friends, talk to them as equals, and engage in extracurricular activities with them to help establish positive relationships.

Our contact with students' families started with an orientation meeting/potluck dinner. Afterward we all participated by putting our chairs in a circle. Each teacher introduced him- or herself and talked a bit about his or her academic plans for the year. Then we went around the circle, with the students introducing themselves and their families, including siblings.

What purpose did this serve? Alienation and fear of the unknown were removed from our school culture. On this first night, parents checked out all the students at the school and the teachers and administrators as well. They were often surprised to have something to do at orientation besides sit and listen. The students got their first glimpse of the school, with lots of looking at each other as well as some tentative or slightly awkward conversations. The returning students were excited to see each other, but everyone made an effort to make the new families comfortable while they served themselves dinner, moved furniture, introduced themselves, and even helped with the dishes.

In addition to the family orientation meeting, we used a similar model throughout the year to engage the families as a whole in the schooling of their teenagers. The following activities are standard procedure at most schools. But at our school, because of our small size, the administrators and teachers could make personal contact with every parent who participated.

*Open house*: Held in midwinter—parents followed their student's class schedule for an abbreviated school day in the evening.

*Parent information meetings*: Held several times a year—we had talks and discussions on issues of parental concern, such as drug use, possible school expansion, different learning styles, the creative process, and so on.

*Performance night*: Showcase of student works, music, poetry, art, and dance.

*Awards night*: Everyone got an award, a paper plate designed by teachers, sometimes humorous but always affirming the student's best qualities. Teachers received them from students as well. Parents, siblings, and the whole school enjoyed the event.

In the traditional high school setting, with schools averaging fifteen hundred to two thousand students, parents can feel even more alienated at school than the students. Educators are aware of the need for family involvement in the education of their teenagers, but find implementation impossible given the sheer numbers of parents. "Back to school" night at one of these institutions can be a dreadful experience of sitting in a packed auditorium listening to perfunctory speeches given by harried administrators. From there it's on to locating distant classrooms with a thousand other confused parents, listening to a teacher describe the curriculum for a few short minutes, and racing on to the next room in time for the bell. Parents need personal conversations with the teachers about their child, not two-hour marathons without personal contact.

## Stressing Kindness

We believe that great care should be taken in promoting the right human relationships among teenagers. This is why our school handbook contained a section that emphasized kindness. You might think it's a corny idea. What kid pays attention to a silly student handbook? Stressing kindness is not a corny idea when we realize that the lack of kindness and mutual respect among teens are the sources of many of the school problems we described in Chapter 1.

We insisted that our students treat each other kindly. We carefully moderated class discussions to ensure respectful interactions. We encouraged differences of opinions, but did not allow personal affronts. Some of our students had never made the distinction between these two approaches. When new students came into class and joined into our discussions, they often would use "put-downs" to make a point. In order to set a standard for kind and thoughtful interactions, a teacher might ask the new student, "Can you make that point as strongly without making fun of someone else's opinion?" or perhaps, "We are respectful of each other's opinions here. We are all interested in Jim's opinion as well as yours." Personal slights were not overlooked but pointed out and corrected. Our goal was fostering a culture of mutual respect.

## Taming Hostility

Whenever fights, hassles, or verbal confrontations arose between students, we used the technique of mediation to tone down the hostility and bring the issue to an acceptable resolution. This system worked very well because it allowed both parties to have their say while promoting an atmosphere of mutual respect. It was also set up to bring closure to the issue in a way that did not necessarily make either party right or wrong, as in this example:

Lyle's active and expressive nature made it hard for him to stay in his chair during class. He often fidgeted, talked out of turn, and inevitably got on the nerves of Rob, the calm and collected poet/artist who didn't have much tolerance for "uncoolness." Rob dealt with Lyle's erratic behavior by criticizing him and continually pointing out his shortcomings. One day during a midmorning class, Lyle had finally had enough of Rob's chiding and leaped out of his chair, challenging him to a fight on the spot. Rob deftly sidestepped Lyle's aggressive approach and the teacher immediately sent them both to the office to work it out with the administrator on duty.

Richard was working the office that morning so he took both boys out onto the lawn to have a chat and mediate the issue. While Rob remained calm, Lyle couldn't get control of himself and cried as he told his side of the story. When Rob's turn came to speak, Lyle repeatedly interrupted and made the mediation very difficult. Richard gently but firmly reminded him of the ground rules of allowing the other side to have his say without being challenged.

Finally both sides of the story were out and Lyle had calmed down enough to proceed to the next step, which was deciding what to do to resolve the problem. Richard asked each boy what he could do to avoid future confrontations and they both agreed that they would alter their behavior. Lyle agreed to work on not interrupting so much in class and Rob agreed not to criticize Lyle. They decided to meet again in a week to see if the agreement was working out. The week went by and the two stuck to their agreement and we had no further problems between them.

## Encouraging Bonding

We felt it was very important for our students to get acquainted outside the confines of the classroom. Going on a weekend camping trip as early in the year as possible allowed them to mix together in a nonacademic environment. Apart from the basic requirements of helping prepare three meals a day and building a campfire every evening, students were allowed to organize their own activities. There were impromptu hikes, touch football games, swimming and surfing (if we were camped at the beach), and a lot of just hanging out in their tents and getting to know each other. While we did make sure that everyone was treating each other kindly, the kids seemed to naturally bond and formalize their own ways of communicating and forming friendships.

We also ended the year with a camping trip, and one of the activities on the last night was to gather around the campfire and honor each student for his or her fine points and positive traits. One of our teachers would go all the way around the circle, honoring each person, and then anyone else could confer his or her own honors.

These trips helped promote right human relations by allowing the students to form friendships on their own terms and make connections in a relaxed and supportive atmosphere.

**Noncompetitive Games**

The entire school participated in occasional coed baseball games that were the result of a spontaneous trip to the park or a planned event. We urged all teachers and students to play. One student had a temporary condition that kept him from running, so another student volunteered to run for him when he was up to bat. The teachers played, the true athletes and the clumsiest ones played, even the girl who didn't want to break her nails played. The defeats were soothed and the triumphs cheered. It was fun for the kids who were not gifted athletically and sometimes a challenge for those who had played competitive sports to tone down their aggression. One hot shot ballplayer did not want to be on a team with girls and teachers who might lose the game for him. He kept trying to stack a team with the best players, but the fun-lovers outnumbered him.

In all of these games we were utterly respectful of our students. At times some students who tried to manipulate our kindness to their advantage saw this as a weakness. They tested us as teenagers do, but we insisted on *mutual* respect. The staff demanded the same respect they lavished on the students.

Students who transferred from public schools told us that the interpersonal culture on their former campuses was quite different from ours. These differences included cliques who rejected and snubbed outsiders, students who "dissed" (showed disrespect) each other, bullying, and tormenting teachers.

## TEACHERS WHO DRAW OUT GENIUS

As teachers and parents we can acknowledge that no matter what teenagers are exhibiting on the surface, be it hostility, aggression, noncommitment, or passivity, each one of them has an inner light that he or she is longing to have recognized. When we approach students with compassion, caring, and kindness, when we show them respect and listen to what they are saying, we begin to encourage that inner light to shine.

When children are treated badly at school, bullied, ridiculed, or made to feel inferior, they erect defense mechanisms that over time can block out their feelings of inner goodness. Much in the same way that we wrap ourselves in heavy blankets when we feel cold, children use the defenses of withdrawal, denial, and anger for comfort from the hostile environment. Over time these heavy blankets can significantly reduce their ability to feel good about themselves, because the inner light isn't able to shine through these outer defenses. But this process can be reversed and in a nurturing and nonthreatening environment the defenses can be laid aside.

## Teachers Who Recognize Genius

Teachers who look beyond the surface to see the potential in their students give them the confidence to be themselves. Our efforts to educate teenagers will be strengthened when we have supportive teachers who practice tolerance for each student's unique way of self-expression:

The bad news about the state of the world was depressing the students in Marilyn Mosley's environmental studies class. She listened and encouraged them when they said they wanted to do something about it. She told them they could make a difference.

The handful of ordinary kids decided to create a video examining issues such as global warming and ozone depletion in the atmosphere. They had no filmmaking experience and using a borrowed video camera their initial efforts were fraught with technical problems such as poor sound, poor lighting, and jiggling images.

But instead of getting discouraged they persevered with constant encouragement from Marilyn. Collaboration with a professional filmmaker ultimately resulted in a superb twenty-minute video that was warm, poignant, and technically perfect. With a script and music written and performed by the students, it really delivered the message they wanted to convey about their concern for the planet. They called the video "You Can Make a Difference."

They decided to raise the money to take the video to Geneva, Switzerland, and present it to the United Nations headquarters. This was a very ambitious project for a handful of teens, but Marilyn continued to assure them they could accomplish anything. By the end of the school year they were on their way to Europe with their video. They had absolutely no contacts at the UN and when they arrived in Geneva they approached the guard at the gate and asked him to deliver the video to the proper department.

The next morning they received a call that their video was a big hit and a UN official wanted to introduce them to her colleagues and give them a tour of headquarters. The video "You Can Make a Difference" won a Global 500 Award from the United Nations and continues to be shown many years after it was made.

Marilyn's belief in her students and her unremitting quest to draw out their best qualities resulted in an incredible demonstration of initiative and creativity to achieve an altruistic goal. Marilyn was demonstrating and confirming by her belief in her students that they could accomplish anything. She was helping them give substance to their dreams.

We don't expect every teacher to take his or her class to Europe, but the willingness to help students bring their ideas into manifestation empowers teens. A good teacher cares.

Teachers can also draw out self-expression by providing a variety of methods for students to demonstrate what they have learned in any given subject. This might include artistic or visual expression of the material, giving a speech, or even creating a skit to demonstrate learning:

The history teacher was having a difficult time getting another of his classes interested and involved in studying the history of England. He knew he had a number of actors in the class and decided to let them dramatize various periods from that history in small plays that they wrote themselves. The first such dramatization involved the trial of King Charles I. The students created a court scene complete with judge, jury, and witnesses. They invented intrigue and suspense and a twist at the end.

They next dramatized the lives of English philosophers Thomas Hobbes and John Locke with interesting and often hilarious results. These presentations allowed the students to learn about history with the goal of demonstrating their learning in a way they enjoyed. They retained the information much more comprehensively than they would have from a lecture.

## Teachers Walk a Fine Line

Teens love teachers who are energetic and imaginative. They like to hear stories that relate to the subject at hand. They like being treated fairly and don't mind teachers who maintain order so long as they don't resort to rudeness or anger as a controlling device. It is essential that high school teachers possess some kind of affinity for the worldview of teenagers. That being said, they must also tread a fine line between identifying with the teen point of view and maintaining their own position as the person in charge.

There should be no question about who's in charge in the classroom and what the rules of behavior are. Teachers who stressed kindness and respect and then followed through by exhibiting those traits themselves were the most effective teachers at our school. But at times we had teachers who became so chummy with their students that they lost their perspective about the balance that must be struck between youthful exuberance and the limits that should be placed on that exuberance. At other times we had well-meaning and basically kind teachers who had their own notions about what constituted proper classroom management. They were either too authoritative or too condescending or just plain rude to the students.

As administrators we always listened to what the students said about their teachers, and if we began to get numerous negative reports we would collect as much information as possible and then sit down with the teacher and go over the issues that had come up. This procedure nearly always resulted in improvements in the way these teachers related to their students. Most of them appreciated the feedback and endeavored to change their approach. We always attempted to deal with teacher issues kindly and fairly, with as much open communication as possible. The success of this approach is detailed in the following story:

We were pleased to have Edward as our new math teacher. He'd been raised and educated in England and had good qualifications, a pleasant appearance, and experience with teenagers. We thought he was going to be great and were happy to have him, as good math teachers are hard to find. With his accent and charming manner we thought the students would be delighted as well.

We were surprised when students started grumbling about their new, "stuck up" math teacher. Of all things, they said he was being rude to them. We met with Edward to talk it over and he said that in his schooling in Great Britain, teachers were expected to project that kind of attitude. Edward was very interested in learning exactly what was offending his students and told us that he had received similar complaints about his teaching style before he came to our school. He was eager to make the necessary adjustments. He changed his posturing and was delighted by the resulting receptivity and praise from his students.

## SCHOOL ENVIRONMENT CAN DRAW
## OUT GENIUS

Because we stressed kindness, tolerance, and respect at our school, our students were relaxed and much more confident about expressing their creative inclinations. We promoted a campus culture in which self-expression was strongly encouraged. The students responded to this encouragement with joy and exuberance and we seldom heard complaints about the school day being too long or the classes boring. The culture of kindness and tolerance helped the students develop a fondness for the school and a desire to spend time there. One thing that we did to help our students relax and begin to express their inner goodness was not to be too restrictive about how they dressed or wore their hair:

Most of our students transferred into our school from the public schools and occasionally they were very quiet and shy. It was often difficult to get them to relax and open up. One student in particular, named Helen, appeared very insecure during her entire first year at our school. She clung to an older classmate whom she'd known before enrolling and was painfully unable to integrate into the social environment of the school. Her "look" when she began school was one of deliberate plainness, as if she were trying to blend into the background.

But by the second year she was obviously becoming more comfortable with expressing herself and she came to school one day with her hair up in a tight French twist, wearing a dark sheath dress. En route to her English class Helen passed one of her teachers, stopped for a moment, and then whispered to her, "Audrey Hepburn."

From there Helen's appearance went through some wonderful and amazing transformations as she became more confident and outspoken. She cut her hair, dyed it red, wore outrageous eye makeup and slinky dresses, all the while getting top grades and developing a unique artistic expression. After high school she gained admission to the University of California and graduated as an art major with an emphasis in photography.

### The Creative Process

The creative process is not just about art and music. It is the process we use to come up with solutions to every kind of issue faced in life, including dilemmas we may encounter in business, medicine, science, as well as the arts. What the marketplace demands these days is not a person who will do exactly as he or she is told, memorize the instructions, and repeat the task endlessly. Employers want someone with good "people" and communication skills who can meet with others in the department to discuss problems and challenges and come up with innovative, cost-effective, workable solutions and then be able to implement them efficiently.

A study cited by Daniel Goleman in his book *Emotional Intelligence*, conducted at the prestigious Bell Labs in Princeton, New Jersey, found that the "star performers"—the engineers who consistently produced the best results—were the ones who had established a rapport with a network of key people they could rely on to help them brainstorm solutions to technical problems. Other engineers with greater intellectual abilities but lacking well-developed communication skills didn't excel because they couldn't easily tap the wide network of minds needed to solve the complex problems encountered in electrical technology.

The creative process is the other essential element needed for successful problem solving. Good communication skills combined with the creative process can provide teenagers with the tools they need to succeed. We taught the fundamentals of the creative process each year so that students could put it into practice in their lives. We believe this four-step creative process is integral to how we educate teenagers:

1. *An initial interest*: Interest in the subject is a must. The student researches everything he or she can on the subject from as many sources as possible—people, books, videos, and so on.

2. *The saturation point*: This point is reached when the student just wants to get away from the subject—take a break. One student called it "getting in the hammock."

3. *The "Aha!" or an idea strikes*: This could happen in the shower, on the bus to school, or while doing the dishes. The student gets an inspiration out of the blue, an idea for the theme paper, and writes it down.

4. *Getting it done*: The student puts the idea into form, writes the paper, paints the painting, prepares the presentation for the class, whatever.

The application of the creative process is not always obvious in the school environment so here's an example of how it could be applied:

1. *To engage creative responses from students, a teacher must generate enough interest or excitement to have them want to look more deeply at an issue.* We have to find a way to let a student who is passionate about something delve into it fully. We can do this by helping stu-

dents choose projects that interest them, helping them find resources outside of school, and giving some of our teaching time outside of class.

This first step of immersing one's self in a subject may be a problem in a class like English literature, where students only get a smattering of short selections. The standardized curriculum that most school districts follow sets out course material that a teacher must cover in order for his or her students to score well on standardized tests. His or her teaching skills are often judged by how well the students score on these tests. With these testing demands, how can students go into depth with a subject that they are truly interested in? Here's an example of how a teacher used the first step of the creative process to stimulate a student's interest in literature:

When they read a short story by William Faulkner in the American literature class, most students found the never-ending sentences tiresome and the Civil War South less than compelling. But Adrienne was an intense and well-read student who felt passionate about the characters and flew through the language. Ellen suggested a few titles she could read outside of class. Adrienne wanted to conduct an in-depth analysis of an aspect of the women in Faulkner's books and she wanted to talk to Ellen about it. They met after school twice a week. She wrote an impressive paper and received extra English credit for her independent study.

2. *After conducting their research, we encouraged our students to take some time to put the project aside.* This is the second step in the creative process and the one most often overlooked. We don't honor "loafing" very much in our society. Doing nothing is a somewhat revolutionary idea, because most teenagers' lives are, as one teen put it, "scheduled into oblivion" with sports, part-time jobs, homework, dance or self-defense classes, family obligations, and dating. When do they lie in the grass and look up at the sky through an overhead tree? When do they have a chance to ruminate over and assimilate all of the new ideas and information they have been learning? New ideas require this time of gestation. If we are constantly on the run, innovation will be hard to come by.

Students need to know the value of this "down time" to allow creative inspirations to germinate. So, for example, if a teen has deeply researched a project but is not coming up with a good idea or angle for the paper, he or she should be encouraged to take a walk in the fresh air and forget about it for a while.

3. *With a little distance from the problem, an idea usually comes.* Ideas strike with incessant regularity in the teenage mind. Teens have some problems turning these ideas into personal success for several reasons. They don't have any frame of reference to judge the value of their ideas due to lack of life experience and limited education. They are rarely asked to even articulate their thoughts. They have not learned to pay attention to the thoughts that cross their minds.

When teaching the creative process to teenagers we repeatedly stressed the importance of listening to their own thoughts and recording them in diaries, notebooks, journals, and sketchpads. This process gives teens a chance to reflect upon their own inspirations. The most important part of this third step in the creative process for teens is to record the inspiration when it comes.

4. *Getting it done is the last step in the creative process.* We have found that many students are reluctant to write or speak because they don't know what to say, or they think that what they have to say is not valuable. When we tell students to "write that paper because it's due tomorrow" and they procrastinate, we should go over the steps in the creative process with them to confirm whether they are *ready* to get it done. Have they researched? Have they stepped back from the project for a while? Do they have an idea to develop? If not, they should go back; if so, they can go forward.

Getting it done just takes some perseverance. Teenagers are notoriously short on perseverance. They are learning to deal with distractions, budget their time, prepare their materials, and identify the steps needed to complete a project. Any help parents and teachers can give them to stick with it, finish the project well, and feel the satisfaction of a task completed is a great gift to students. It helps them look forward to the next task and feel confidence in their growing abilities. If we, in any way, do the project for them, we are really stealing this satisfaction from them. We can guide them but not put words in their mouths. It is a delicate balancing act that parents and teachers have to engage in. We put intense effort into this last step in the process, the getting it done, because life is lived by doing it, not just having an idea.

Some schools have adopted a *portfolio model* of assessment rather than testing. Students are assessed by the body of work they present as their portfolio, which is arranged to show a picture of a student's development and mastery of a subject. This type of assessment is familiar to fine arts teachers but is now being used more for academic disciplines as well. For instance, in a chemistry portfolio a student might have to solve a problem, design an experiment, analyze a result, defend a position, and critique a current event. This form of assessment holds students accountable for more than factual recall. The focus in the portfolio is on what the student has accomplished in the form of creative work.

### Activities That Encourage Self-Expression

There are many activities that can be offered during the school day to break up the monotony and promote creativity and self-expression. Students should be encouraged to express themselves during these appropriately supervised events so that they feel their opinions are being acknowledged. They need to feel that they are part of the vital life of the school and that their opinions and creative expressions are valuable. The following are three ways we encouraged self-expression at our school:

1. *Encourage two-way communications during school assemblies.* We initially used our weekly assemblies to pass out permission slips, make announcements, and so forth. But these affairs quickly became so perfunctory and boring that we decided to liven them up. We formed a "Joy Committee" that encouraged the students to express their creativity by reading original poetry, playing musical compositions, or just announcing something fun or important that they'd done the previous week. We also used the assemblies to present token awards to students who had guessed the source of the daily quote, which was always posted in front of the school office. These opportunities to express themselves and have fun made the assemblies much more of an interactive affair and cut down dramatically on the boredom factor.

2. *Organize "performance nights" in which every student can participate.* Our performance nights definitely wouldn't have won any Academy Awards, and that is just the point. These events weren't about being the best and brightest, they were about encouraging creativity and applauding every effort, no matter how rough around the edges. Giving students a chance to perform before an audience raised their self-esteem and confidence by encouraging every effort to be creative. These events featured original music, dramatic skits and readings, poetry, and premier showings of student films. The entire student body and many families and guests turned out for the performance nights, which took place in a rented hall. They were events that everyone

looked forward to and they really brought the school together as a creative unit.

3. *Use music to promote creativity.* Music classes provide an avenue for teens to express themselves. Our music program was always popular because we allowed the students to concentrate on the music they liked. It invariably occurred that some kind of rock band emerged from the class, which certainly made our performance nights more exciting. Here's a story about one of our music teachers who possessed infectious creativity:

One year we were blessed with an extraordinary music and physics teacher named Paul. In addition to being a gifted guitarist and drummer, Paul was also familiar with the Australian didgeridoo, a wind instrument that produces a melodic droning sound. He immediately connected with the students and elicited excitement, enthusiasm, and dedication from them.

Paul organized an afterschool drumming circle at a nearby park and his students brought along their friends and even some moms and dads. Through this effort Paul really made a breakthrough with one student with whom he was having particular trouble with in his physics class. The drumming provided a bond that transformed this student's attitude from one of antagonism to close friendship.

But Paul's greatest contribution was getting his students involved in playing the didgeridoo. He taught them an easy way to make these traditional instruments out of inexpensive PVC pipe. He provided the materials and instruction and soon the school was alive with the rumbling rhythm and droning sounds of Aboriginal music. Making their own didgeridoos and then learning how to play them provided a positive and creative way that the students could channel their energy.

## TWENTY QUESTIONS FOR PARENTS

1. How often do you acknowledge your teenager's gifts, talents, intelligence, and attributes?

2. Do you overlook the tough exterior and compassionately address the struggling teenager inside?

3. As a parent are you helping your child to achieve self-discovery or imposing your own expectations?

4. How is your teen's high school addressing his or her inherent intelligence and gifts?

5. Is your teenager being acknowledged for his or her contribution at school in any way besides grades?

6. Is your teenager given a voice in school decisions such as choice of classes or extracurricular activities, or are choices made by the school or parents?

7. Have your teenager's teachers given him or her some authority over school projects that acknowledge student capability?

8. Do any of your teenager's teachers have a positive relationship with your child outside of school?

9. Are you comfortable enough at your teenager's school to have relaxed conversations with teachers and staff?

10. Would "kindness" be considered one of the main qualities in your teenager's school culture?

11. What is the procedure at your teenager's high school for dealing with hostility? Do students learn anything or just "get in trouble"?

12. Are there opportunities for students to form friendships outside of the classroom, such as camping trips, hikes, all-school games, and sports?

13. Do you feel your teenager's life is enhanced or diminished by participation in competitive sports?

14. Does your teenager have a teacher who is willing to help bring his or her ideas into manifestation?

15. Have you ever heard your teenager express disrespect for a teacher who can't maintain order in the class?

16. Is your teenager's school environment one that promotes self-expression?

17. Do you wholeheartedly support your teenager's completion of a creative project or interest in a subject such as a musical instrument?

18. When your teen wants to laze around and daydream, do you allow him or her this time to process all the new learning or germinate an inspiration?

19. Do your teen's teachers go the extra mile to help him or her explore an intellectual passion or area of interest?

20. Does the high school your teen attends put any energy into drawing out the special "genius" of each child or is it committed to teaching them all a set block of information?

## CHAPTER FOUR

# The New Curriculum

Education is the kindling of a flame, not the filling of a vessel.
—Aristotle

In this chapter we will enable parents to explore a curriculum that can draw out excellence from students. By teaching standard subjects in different styles and encouraging experiential learning, we prepared our students for the very best. Our graduates attended Harvard University, Bennington College, and various campuses of the University of California. Some were admitted on scholarships to these venerable institutions and to smaller schools such as Suffolk College in Massachusetts and Green Mountain College in Vermont. Other graduates became media specialists, auto mechanics, carpenters, professional pianists, doctor's assistants, sculptor's apprentices, graphic artists, and actors. Our school enrolled the truly learning-disabled right along with students with the highest Scholastic Aptitude Test (SAT) scores in the nation—students who received the Presidential Scholar Award based on SAT scores. How was this accomplished?

Although we were an alternative school, we followed the state-mandated curriculum so that our students could satisfy all college entrance requirements. But we taught these standard subjects in a very different way, which we will discuss in depth in this chapter. What we wanted to do was show kids how to explore a subject, how to develop a love for learning, how to go toward something rather than having it pushed at them.

We recognize that there are many teenagers who are not academically inclined, but nonetheless are vibrant, lively, and have a rich perspective on life. We always endeavored to teach to the entire range of abilities, excluding no one. There was no such thing as a special education class at our school. If we teach how to think, how to learn, how to discriminate and discern, how to create and produce, we can prepare high school students for any field or to continue their education if they choose.

## WHAT TO TEACH

Teenagers are at a critical juncture in their lives, with so much of their future uncertain. Unknowns abound as their hormones kick in and, at the same time, so much is expected of them. They need adult friends and advisers. They need intimacy and support. They need to have fun and the freedom to experiment and try out their newly developing abilities. And yet they need to get serious about their future. They have to juggle many demands at once.

Is it right to have teens repeating time-consuming tasks at school that have no bearing on their lives? Should we ask them to spend their time studying and passing exams and not even care whether they remember the material the following week? Much of what they are given in school is exactly that. We shouldn't disregard the question they are asking: "What purpose does this serve?"

Everything that we teach to high school students should be pertinent to their lives. We shouldn't teach anything that doesn't have relevance. At our school we were often asked by the students, "How does this information relate to me?" Teachers need to make an effort to present the information so that students see the relevance. A lesson made relevant is also retained longer than a lesson that merely asks students to memorize places, dates, and names of historical figures.

Teachers should attempt to recognize the universal themes in the curriculum material and apply these themes to the contemporary experience:

Dave was among a group of very tough and active boys in the senior English class. They spent much of their time reading and discussing stories related to survival. Jack London's short stories were the students' favorite. When it came time to read more complex works the teacher chose *Gulliver's*

*Travels.* This eighteenth-century classic provided a marvelous way to demonstrate how Swift's satire was applicable to the current political situation
in the world. While reading about the adventures of Samuel Gulliver, Dave
was able to identify the story's relevancy to the universal political themes of
intrigue and pettiness.

The teacher used a combination of teaching aids including videos and
audiotapes to bring the literature alive for the students. In comprehending
Swift's satire, Dave began to recognize the way literature could be used to
make a statement about society. The writing assignments were geared toward drawing out the students' own observations about society and how
important issues could be addressed through stories.

One night Dave was watching the television version of *Gulliver's Travels*
with his parents and impressed them by pointing out the many instances of
political satire in the film. This was a student who rarely read a book and
had shown no interest in the relevancy of literature prior to his twelfth-grade
English class.

## Curriculums Change with the Times

In the nineteenth century the standard curriculum included Latin
and debate. It was designed for the privileged male students who
would never be wage earners. As an example of how things change,
by the 1950s Ellen was attending a mandatory home economics course
for eighth-grade girls. She remembers learning that her hair was her
"crowning glory," how to make applesauce, and how to operate a
sewing machine and sew up a bib apron. The "girls" in her class were
being prepared to be the future homemakers of America. The deciding factor in what is taught has always been an economic one.

What are the current economic pressures on curriculum planning?
What information do we need to pass on to our high school students?
In this information age we are suffering from an information overload.
We are surrounded by information, we might even say "bombarded"
with too much of it. We need to learn how to discriminate, how to
choose the most beneficial information. Some trends in curriculum
design reflect this direction. Unlike the past, when we studied in our
field and then worked in that field for our entire career life, today
learning a specialty has its shortcomings. Most people make several
career changes and work in many jobs rather than one. Graduates need
to learn skills that can be applied broadly.

*Critical thinking* is a skill that is sought after in the current economic climate and emphasized in the more forward-looking curriculums. A mind trained to sift through mountains of material and find

the pertinent information is an asset in today's information-cluttered society. An *integrated curriculum* recognizes that the compartmentalizing that was essential to our earlier curriculum model no longer fits what we know about the world. All of the disciplines impact each other and can no longer be studied in isolation. Chemistry will become part of a study of the physical world. English will be taught as one aspect of communications. World history becomes crucial to the study of community. *Project-based learning* consists of small groups who cooperate and work as a team to create a product such as a video, a business, or an event. Thriving in the new workplace requires shared leadership through sincere cooperation or true teamwork. Top-down leadership has been found to be unproductive in our fast-changing world.

Our school used the standard curriculum as a basis for subject matter but taught the subjects using critical thinking and a project-based curriculum. We attempted to approach each subject holistically and with a broad frame of reference.

## Standard Curriculum

The standard curriculum for high schools as defined by many states includes four years of history and English, three years of science, three years of math, two years of a foreign language, two years of physical education, and a variety of electives including fine arts. When high school students assimilate the body of knowledge contained in this curriculum framework, it becomes the vehicle through which our cultural values are transmitted to them. High school is the culmination of formal education for a significant percentage of the population. For the college-bound it is supposed to lay the foundation for a tertiary education. Either way it's a critical time for learning.

At Mountain View we used the standard curriculum set out by state guidelines as our basic tool. Our school was registered with the county department of education and we selected state-adopted textbooks from the department's curriculum library. But we often wondered how relevant the content of these standard texts was for our students' lives. With the amount of available knowledge exponentially increasing each year, a person can't assimilate even one subject in an entire lifetime. In every field there are new discoveries and changes that make textbooks obsolete before they are printed. Scientists are currently looking at a tenth planet. Carbon dating has lengthened the time span of human history. Transcontinental human migrations are getting pushed further back in time. Even with these reservations about the texts, we wanted our students to be able to satisfy the state's educational requirements and have their transcripts be compatible with those of other high schools.

The scholarly disciplines of mathematics, science, literature, and history encompass the intellectual achievement of our culture. The definition of an educated person in our society is someone who has acquired a basic knowledge in all of these areas. He or she is familiar with the principles of biology, knows who Dickens and Shakespeare were, is able to compute and calculate, and can probably relate the causes of the two major wars of the twentieth century. Every citizen should have the opportunity to learn about the world in this disciplined way.

Teens should be able to assimilate the body of knowledge taught in high school and it should be appropriate for their level of intellectual ability. Even though relevancy should be at the top of the list when formulating a curriculum, unfortunately it isn't. Every current discussion of what is taught as "the curriculum" now has to consider if it will prepare the student for testing. Testing has become the driving force in the creation of many high school curriculums.

## Standardized Testing

Nearly every school requires students to sit down with a list of questions or problems to solve in order to demonstrate learning. Most high schools also administer standardized achievement tests. Nineteen states now require exit exams for high school diplomas and many colleges require entrance exams.

But most of these tests only measure a student's ability to recall and recite facts, and much of what is learned, such as leadership and innovation, is not acknowledged. Standardized tests leave little room for individualized or creative responses. Colleges are realizing this problem and are becoming less reliant on entrance exams such as the national Scholastic Aptitude Test (SAT). As has been reported in the media, a number of prominent colleges are dropping the SAT requirement for incoming freshmen.

At the same time, the federal government has passed legislation to impose standardized testing across the nation starting in the third grade. Politicians and educators hope to put an end to educational woes by standardizing a body of knowledge for the entire United States and then testing for competency. Those who pass go to college; those who don't won't.

According to an article by CNN correspondent Bill Delaney titled "Critics Fear State Test Taking Will Take Its Toll," the state of Massachusetts is requiring tenth graders to pass a proficiency exam before being granted a diploma. He said the test could jeopardize college plans for a great many high school students. Delaney quoted the principal of Boston's Fenway High School, who said that dozens of his best students might be accepted by various colleges but be unable to attend because they didn't pass the state exam. Principal Larry Myatt said the statewide test doesn't measure creativity, teamwork, research skills, and many other ways in which learning can be demonstrated.

Myatt gave the example of a senior who graduated in 2001 from Fenway. The son of Haitian immigrants and a student standout who received a full scholarship to Franklin Pierce College in New Hampshire, he failed the state exam in tenth grade before passing it became mandatory. Myatt said that linking the granting of diplomas to passing a test will be a blow to the confidence of many otherwise successful students and could eventually discourage them from taking the test over again if they fail.

He feared that "teaching to the test" will become the educational norm. He said he's having a hard time "getting behind something that's going to keep some of my best and brightest out of college." Other critics of the mandatory testing say the tests will end up measuring mostly those best prepared for the exams, not those best prepared for college, work, or life.

## Testing Is Not the Best Way to Demonstrate Learning

We agree that every student should be exposed to a standard core curriculum, but each teacher will teach it differently, and each student will hear and think about it differently. Each teacher and every student should be encouraged to bring their unique capabilities, history, culture, and previous education to the task.

We maintain that knowledge is not static or stable and that testing must reflect this. What about students who demonstrate their learning through projects or verbally rather than through the standard written format? Will they be excluded from tertiary education? What about immigrant children and artistic children—are they not qualified for higher education? Also, many students excel in one area but do not have the aptitude for another. Will we be doing candidates for college a service by eliminating those who could excel in a specialty, say mathematics, but can't wrap their mind around literature and therefore fail the language aspect of the standardized tests?

The testing itself poses questions. In a typical ninety-minute math test, how can twenty or thirty test items delivered in multiple choice and short answers cover all the math learned during a high school career? Just as one book does not represent a library, so the short standardized test cannot represent math competency.

When the results of a test have severe consequences, such as teachers losing their jobs and schools losing their funding, educators will find a way to enable their students to do better on that test. Teachers will narrow their curriculum to meet the test, which is referred to as "teaching to the test." And teachers will spend class time teaching test-taking skills, which increase scores. More time will be spent giving repeated tests, which has been shown to increase test scores. Will these measures benefit the student? Will the student learn more about math or about taking tests?

During the 1980s in Great Britain, the Thatcher government experimented with national standardized testing, which prompted a successful teacher boycott in 1990. The disadvantages reported by a consensus of teachers were a curriculum narrowed to the core subjects and core material focused primarily on the test. British teachers also said that special needs children were suffering from the reestablishment of skill and ability groupings aimed at raising test scores among the more advanced students. Overall the teachers found the national testing scheme detrimental to constructive learning and teaching.

At Mountain View, testing did not drive the curriculum. Teachers aimed for student mastery of understanding as opposed to recognition of right answers. Some students needed extra time to take a test; some students were given the option of oral exams or producing a project to demonstrate their learning.

A portfolio assessment in which a student collects and presents his or her learning is being used more widely in high schools to demonstrate learning. Many colleges are accepting portfolios as part of submission for acceptance. Portfolios are not easily standardized, but they build students' ownership and confidence in their learning. Students can see themselves getting smarter through the progress of their work throughout the year. When we make kids show what they know, sometimes they surprise themselves:

In tenth-grade English, Serena was assigned a portfolio project for the study of Shakespeare's *Richard III*. She needed to make an entry in her portfolio every night. The entries were to reflect the topics covered in class, such as an introduction to "The Bard," the definition of tragedy and comedy, character studies of the cast, and contemporary translations of Richard's opening and closing monologues.

At first it all sounded like a huge writing assignment, but the portfolio became a sensory experience. Pictures cut from magazines personified the cast of characters. The colored background paper for Richard's closing speech matched the mood of the monologue. The comedy and tragedy masks illustrated the precise definition of a Shakespearean tragedy. Photos of the Tower of London, a setting in the play, printed from the Internet enhanced the historical feeling, and an Elizabethan etching of the wild boar from Richard's family crest illustrated the family tree.

Serena's portfolio, which contains an intense and persistent study of *Richard III,* is hers to look at in the future and enjoy. The play is indelibly etched into her memory because she was a participant rather than an observer. And certainly the portfolio demonstrated her learning as well as a "twenty-page paper due in three weeks" or a multiple choice/short answer test.

## LEARNING HOW TO LEARN

What does this mean, learning how to learn? We can't assume that teenagers know how to assimilate and retain knowledge. Many of the teenagers we encountered had no idea how to study. The first question we have to ask is, "How do they learn best?" After we get rid of the fear and the barriers to learning through providing a safe campus, what are we left with? Let us assume that the students are comfortable, feeling safe and supported by the school environment. The task of learning the subjects is in front of them. Are they equipped to tackle algebra, civics, or a foreign language? Learning how to learn has to be part of the curriculum.

### Start with the Physical: Is Everything Functioning?

Many students have learning difficulties that can be easily remedied with some personal attention. But in a large class of thirty-five students, will a teacher know that a particular student isn't wearing his or her glasses and therefore can't see the chalkboard? There were students at Mountain View who would not wear their glasses because they didn't look cool. We worked with our students and their parents to overcome many other personal barriers to learning, such as the following:

- Students with tiny earphones in their ears and a CD player hidden in their laps
- Students who drink highly caffeinated soft drinks and then can't sit still
- Students who don't get enough sleep
- Students who are hungry

Learning is impossible without correction of these situations and personal attention from us. The maturity level is in such a state of flux during the teen years that attention to these seemingly small things makes a big difference. How can Melissa learn algebra if she can't see the board, is distracted by hunger, and keeps falling asleep?

## Learn How You Learn

Let's say you want to learn how to surf. You could watch a video, have someone tell you how to do it, or paddle out into the waves and learn by trial and error. We have just described three potential ways of learning: visual, verbal, and kinesthetic. We all have the ability to learn by seeing, by being told, and through physical practice. But each of us would probably favor one of these ways of learning over the other options.

Being a strongly verbal person, Ellen can only learn something when she concentrates on the meaning of the words. She does this best in complete silence with no distractions. On the other hand, our son always had the radio blaring when he was doing his homework. And he moved around so much that it's a wonder he got anything written down. He is kinesthetic and musical.

In order to discover how our students learned best, we gave them a "Self-Portrait Profile" on the first day of school to determine their individual learning styles. This test, developed by two educators, Mariaemma Pelullo Willis and Victoria Hodson, consists of a series of provocative self-scoring questions and five categories in which to apply the scores: writer, artist, thinker, producer, and performer, or a combination of any two of the five. The categories that received the most points revealed the particular learning style.

The students enjoyed this test because it was all about them and their learning preferences. When we were curious about a particular student we could look in the file for this information to help us better understand his or her academic inclinations. But most of the time, all it took was observation to determine how a student learned. The highly dramatic and talkative person learned by performing; the one who always had his or her head down doodling learned through artistic projects and videos. The discovery of learning styles can be accomplished through observation and common sense.

We wanted our students to do well, and because we were a small school we could get to know all of them. As teachers we responded to what brought fire into their eyes. When we first read Dr. Howard Gardner's *Notes on Multiple Intelligences* in 1980, describing his work at the Harvard School of Education on the theory of multiple intelligences, it codified and confirmed for us what we were already doing. We had a diverse group of kids and they taught us that there are various kinds of learning methods. Our task was to identify each student's learning style and teach to him or her in that style for at least a portion of each class session. The following are questions that should be asked when trying to determine learning styles of students:

- Do they learn by watching and imitating?
- Do they learn by practicing it over and over until they get it right?
- Do they learn by having someone carefully explain each step to them?
- Do they learn by recognizing the rhythm of things?
- Do they learn by imagining?
- Do they learn by intuiting?
- Do they learn by discussing and sharing?

## Seven Kinds of Smart

We believe that high school students will assimilate more knowledge if they can do it in a way that best matches their proclivity for learning. Unfortunately, in most high school and college classrooms, learning is pursued by a teacher standing in front of a group of students and lecturing to them. The students are supposed to be busily taking notes and not talking.

This is a model designed for a student with linguistic intelligence, which is sensitivity to the sounds, structure, meanings, and functions of words and language. The student with this kind of intelligence thinks in words, loves reading and writing, and learns best through books, audiotapes, and dialogue. Our society honors linguistic and logical intelligence above all else, and linguistic intelligence has formed the essence of education in our culture. Classroom discussions, rather than the lecture format, result in greater retention of information, application of knowledge to new situations, and development of higher-order thinking skills. And yet a majority of high school teachers still use the traditional lecture as their primary instructional method.

Most of our nation's classrooms are set up for verbal and logical children. Kids with especially sharp reading, vocabulary, reasoning, and computational skills do well on tests and zoom to the head of the class. Children whose strengths lie elsewhere—in art, music, dance, mechanical reasoning, social savvy, intuitive perception, or sheer creative imagination—may perform poorly and are often labeled as being "learning disabled," "underachieving," "hyperactive," or simply "unmotivated." Students with bodily kinesthetic or spatial intelligence are often labeled "troublemakers," but if students learn through movement, they have to move.

Even though information about multiple intelligences has been well received by teachers and schools systems for two decades, it has not had a dramatic effect on education because it is too hard to implement into the current educational structure. We can just imagine a high school history teacher going to an "in-service" about multiple intelligences and then returning to his or her classroom of forty unruly kids and a set curriculum. Every hour he or she faces a new group of students. How is this teacher supposed to respond to Sonia's musical intelligence as she taps out a rhythm on the desk with her pencil and John's kinesthetic intelligence, which is making him fidget while he is trying to learn the battles of the Civil War?

Thomas Armstrong's book *7 Kinds of Smart* introduced Dr. Howard Gardner's theory of multiple intelligences to the general public. This theory defines the various proclivities for learning, ranging from logical-mathematical and linguistic to spatial and bodily kinesthetic. The following list of the seven intelligences and the areas of endeavor where they may be found is drawn from the work of Gardner and Armstrong.

*Linguistic*: A sensitivity to the sounds, structure, meanings, and functions of words and language. Lawyers, writers, and poets exhibit this intelligence most effectively.

*Logical-Mathematical*: The capacity to comprehend logical and numerical patterns and conduct complex reasoning. This is the realm of scientists and mathematicians.

*Spatial*: The ability to accurately perceive the visual/spatial world and to maneuver, operate, and learn visually. It relates to skill in using plans, drawings, or maps. Sailors, engineers, architects, surgeons, and artists demonstrate spatial intelligence.

*Musical*: Competence in producing and understanding rhythm, pitch, and timbre and appreciating a variety of musical forms. Musicians, composers, and musicologists possess this intelligence.

*Bodily Kinesthetic*: Physical agility and the ability to handle objects skillfully. Demonstrated by dancers, athletes, and carpenters.

*Interpersonal*: A knack for understanding other people, what motivates them, and how to work cooperatively with them. Politicians, psychologists, ministers, and salespeople draw upon this intelligence.

*Intrapersonal*: Also called emotional intelligence, this is the ability to access one's own emotions and to discriminate between them with a sense of control—a knowledge of one's own strengths and weaknesses. Psychotherapists and spiritual leaders show strength in this area of intelligence.

Here is a brief list of the kinds of learning tools that each of these intelligences adapt to best, reprinted from Thomas Armstrong's work:

*Linguistic*: books, tapes, writing implements, paper, dialogue, discussion

*Logical-Mathematical*: things to explore and think about, science materials, trips to science museum

*Spatial*: art, movies, slides, imagination games, illustrated books, trips to art museum

*Bodily Kinesthetic*: role playing, drama, movement, sports and physical games, hands-on learning

*Musical*: trips to concerts, music playing, making music videos

*Interpersonal*: group games, community activities, apprenticeships

*Intrapersonal*: time alone, self-paced projects, learning choices

## Learning Styles, Teaching Styles

Trying to teach every day to the learning styles of every student in a large classroom would be impossible. But there is a simple method of adapting lesson plans to various learning styles by breaking an hour-long class into three twenty-minute segments. Let's say a teacher has a mix of interpersonal, spatial, and musical learners in a cultural geography class who are studying the Navajo people of Arizona. First the teacher could show a twenty-minute video segment on the traditional Navajo way of life, how they move from one climate zone to another throughout the year to graze their sheep and grow corn. Then the class could spend twenty minutes holding a roundtable discussion about the Navajo culture. The last twenty-minute segment could be devoted to playing Navajo music while the students write a short essay on what they learned.

Here are examples of how to address a variety of learning styles in the core curriculum:

### English

*Logical-Mathematical*: Students are assigned a series of analogies (e.g., "tire is to truck as (a) hoof is to horse, (b) shovel is to rake, (c) hand is to wrist").

*Spatial*: Students create illustrations to accompany written essays (e.g., draw the Globe Theatre when studying Shakespeare).

### Cultural Geography

*Musical*: Each unit is introduced with music from the country or the culture being studied (e.g., play a recording of the Tamari rhythms of Polynesia while studying the cultures of the South Pacific).

### Civics/Economics

*Interpersonal*: The principles of economics are taught by allowing students to create a student business (e.g., a school cafe where student-made products are sold and cultural activities such as poetry readings are offered).

### Science

*Intrapersonal*: Students explore their own feelings and responses to the natural world (e.g., they find a spot outdoors away from each other where they can observe nature and write down impressions of what they observe).

### History

*Bodily Kinesthetic*: A unit of history is taught by allowing students to role-play (e.g., when studying the civil rights movement students are assigned to reenact incidents of discrimination against African Americans).

## GENERALIZE OR SPECIALIZE?

There is currently a movement afoot in the United States to restructure and downsize high schools. Educators are acknowledging the efficacy of smaller high schools and are accomplishing this downsizing by breaking large traditional high schools into academies that focus on a particular subject. This specialization would send Pete, whom we met in Chapter 3, directly to a trade school so he could get on with developing his mechanical skills. The high schools that are magnets for the performing arts began this trend, and we now have high schools that stress science and math and use computer technology as a curriculum. Essentially we are looking at the development of high schools as specialized institutions.

### A Possible Future

When Dr. Howard Gardner in his book *The Disciplined Mind: What All Students Should Understand* considered the future of education in relation to multiple intelligences, he said that "we should move toward the creation of a manageable number of distinct pathways." He proposed the following pathways for a heterogeneous nation like the United States:

*The Canon Pathway* for those who desire a system that features traditional American (and Western) historical and artistic values.

*The Multicultural Pathway* for those who desire to study their own culture and compare it with other groups.

*The Progressive Pathway* for those who respect individual differences and growth and seek to create a school community that embodies democratic values.

*The Technological Pathway* for those who desire immersion in technologies to maintain the competitive edge in the work force.

*The Socially Responsible Pathway* for those who desire to be actively involved in improving the world by focusing on national and global issues that are susceptible to solution.

*The Understanding Pathway* for those who desire to tackle the classical and fundamental questions of existence.

Paul T. Hill, a senior fellow at the Brookings Institution and co-author of *Reinventing Public Education: How Contracting Can Transform American Schools,* says that "schools will be smaller" and "every school will have a clearly defined way of teaching. Some schools will emphasize mastery of facts and skills and others will emphasize exploration and discovery. Some will engage students through art, others through science or math and others through connections with careers."

Breaking large schools into smaller ones is laudable and may in fact be crucial for the survival of our high schools. But too often the downsizing is linked to this idea of specialization. As an example an October 2000 federal granting program for creating smaller, more personalized school settings is funding "career academies." Career schools are cropping up based on such areas as science, computers, and the performing arts. For the latter, we picture all of those young talented dancers and singers hoofing it across a rehearsal stage. They are completely engaged and satisfied, at least in the movie version. This is a catchy idea, but it needs to be scrutinized.

## Specialization Is Not the Goal

The educational task in elementary school is to learn the skills of language and computation. In high school students are expected to refine these skills and assimilate their cultural and scientific heritage. The high school experience should be a well-rounded one followed by specialization in college or at a trade school.

The adolescent years provide an opportunity for teenagers to discover their true potential. In traditional societies these are the years devoted to vision quests, rites of passage, and tribal initiation. In these often wild and unwieldy years, teenagers hold the promise of a fresh approach to the world's problems. It is the time of life to be inspired and to develop altruism and leadership. Teenagers long to broaden their perspective of the world and are preparing to launch themselves into it in one capacity or another.

In Chapter 1, we cited Daniel Goleman's book *Emotional Intelligence* and the research on brain development during the adolescent years (twelve to eighteen). According to Goleman the frontal lobes governing self-control, understanding, and artful response are not yet fully developed in teenagers. In terms of school this biological window presents an opportunity for students to learn appropriate responses to a wide range of experiences as their brains mature to assimilate those experiences. Exposing teens to a variety of challenges and teaching methods will help them to develop both intellectually and emotionally.

We believe that channeling teenagers into schools that specialize in one area of endeavor will not result in a well-balanced education. At Mountain View High School we moved in the opposite direction. We taught the state-adopted curriculum in a variety of ways and didn't limit it, the students, or the faculty to one area of expertise. We feel that every student should be exposed to computers, literature, the arts, lab science, and math and that students should mix with others who have skills and talents they themselves do not possess.

For example, we always had a few "computer techies" who would rather have been at home in the realm of cyberspace than in the real world of school. When they came to school they naturally gravitated toward others who spoke the same language. These students often fit a certain profile: usually shy, imaginative, and bright. They tended to want to stay inside and felt safer socializing in a chat room "online" than in the schoolyard.

If the concept of specialized high schools is adopted on a national scale, we wonder how a whole school of these kids would benefit. A computer high school would have techies socializing only with students who have the same interests. They wouldn't experience a diverse class of students who reflect other interests. They wouldn't get outdoors as much. How would they experience other points of view such as a passion for the environment or the extrovert whose life is full of high drama?

We relished seeing our computer kids beach-camping or serving dinner to the homeless. Their skills were valued and sought out by the other students who needed help solving computer problems and finding research items on the Web. Several of them wrote imaginative science fiction stories for our literary magazine. The entire school benefited by their involvement and friendship.

We had enough computers so that nearly every student in the school could explore cyberspace. People were always giving us computers that were in excellent condition, and we realized that with a little initiative any school could get computers. A specialization only in computers seems like a narrow focus for a high school at a time when talents should be developed in other areas as well.

Now let us look at what the mechanically minded Pete might have missed if he'd gone directly into an auto mechanics trade school. He would have missed the creative, artistic girls at our school who initially pushed his buttons but eventually became his friends and helped him develop patience and tolerance. He would have missed the appreciation he received for his willingness to help fix anything, especially cars for girls. He wouldn't have been exposed to world literature, history, and culture. He would not have been as informed a voter as he is now. He would not have had the experience of going away to college with his high school friends. Years later when Pete came back to visit the campus he was a self-assured, gentle, and competent mechanic. What kind of a person would he be without the well-rounded education he received at Mountain View?

And what of the Mountain View student who went to Harvard? If he had gone to a high-powered prep school, would he have ever had a friend like Pete? Would he have had the opportunity to hear from many points of view? Would his incredible intellect have been tempered by compassion for the less gifted? If he becomes a leader in government or industry, as many Harvard graduates do, would he have been as understanding of the variety of approaches to life's challenges?

## LEARNING THROUGH EXPERIENCE

Adolescence represents a significant shift within the stages of human development. Teens are moving from identification with self and peer group to identification with community and the world. In order to facilitate this shift they need experiences in the world. And as Maria Montessori said, "All learning begins with practical experience." Knowledge is created through transformative, concrete experiences.

The traditional high school tends to isolate teens from real-world experiences rather than gradually moving them into the adult world. Most teens are fenced into a large compound for four years and when they are let out they are supposed to know how to integrate into jobs or college.

We feel that a high school should be open and integrated with the community. Teenagers should learn how to move from the world of the confinement and protection in elementary school into the independence and responsibility of young adulthood. We set out to facilitate this transition with limited work experience/apprenticeships and by encouraging sophomores, juniors, and seniors to attend community college classes to prepare them for the transition to college. We also made service in the community part of our curriculum.

We offered experiential learning in the classroom by not separating students into academic classes according to ability. Classes with mixed ability levels enabled students to experience an intellectual and cultural diversity often absent from typical advanced placement classrooms.

## Experiential Learning

Experiential learning provides a refreshing break from the textbook and lecture format and is very conducive to active learning styles. Experiential learning activities combined with careful note taking and short explanations by the instructor can put nearly all learning styles into practice. When we take students outdoors and let them get their hands dirty, when we expose them to the real world and how it works, both the natural environment and human society, they begin to understand how they fit into the scheme of things.

Mountain View High School offered a natural science program in which one entire day a month was spent outdoors. This daylong laboratory enabled students to study the natural environment while being immersed in it. The teacher used the local watershed to teach plant and animal biology, ecology, and how human actions impact natural systems. They also studied what happens at the edges of the ecological zones, where one habitat blends into another.

Another science teacher invited a local bird rescue group to come to school with live hawks and owls so the students could observe the habits of raptors. They were allowed to examine the birds closely and gained a better understanding of their behavior and characteristics. These experiences made science literally come alive for the students. They had the chance to use all of their senses to comprehend and appreciate the complexity of the natural world.

There is no better way to teach geology than to find a hillside close to school that contains examples of the rocks being studied in class. Our school was ten minutes away from a canyon that had unique geologic features; the students could pick out examples of rocks and were able to discover from them the geologic history of the region.

In civics class we covered the workings of the political system and the students chose a local political topic that interested them. The teacher guided them in how to actively address the issue in the political arena. They chose issues such as the curfew law for teenagers, the locating of a massive landfill near the edge of the community, the problem of traffic congestion in the community, and how to make high school more relevant.

The teacher took them through a process that began with writing letters to the editor of the local newspaper. The student letters were printed in the paper and a reporter came out to the school to interview the class. The teacher provided them with tips on how they should prepare themselves for talking to the media. This visit provided students with the opportunity to learn how to articulate their views orally.

The next step involved contacting local, state, and national legislators. These public officials always responded to the students and gave them feedback that they could analyze to determine whether their lobbying had made an impact on the decision-making process. At times they also conducted public opinion polls and went downtown with clipboards and a series of questions they had developed. They learned how to formulate effective survey questions and tabulate the replies and came up with statistics on how the average citizen felt about various political issues.

When teaching a unit on the U.S. Constitution, the goal was to get the students actively involved in the material and not just have them passively listening to lectures or memorizing the various sections of the document. This was achieved by creating a "Supreme Court" simulation in which the students acted as lawyers for a constitutional case involving teenagers. They were to defend an imaginary young man who'd had his constitutional rights violated and research the Bill of Rights to come up with breaches of the various amendments to defend their client. They also drew upon previous Supreme Court decisions that had set precedents supporting their defense.

On the day the cases were to be heard the class divided into lawyers and Supreme Court justices, with the teacher presiding as chief justice. The students worked in pairs to defend their cases before the panel of judges and their performances were evaluated following a rating sheet supplied to the student justices. The exercise stimulated student interest in the Constitution as they experienced being lawyers and using the document as a defense. They embraced the material and felt empowered to have learned about their own constitutional rights.

## Work Experience and Apprenticeships

We encouraged our juniors and seniors to pursue part-time jobs and under certain conditions gave them elective credit. For instance, one senior who planned to attend a teacher training college worked as a teacher's aide at the nearby elementary school. She had an afternoon break in her academic schedule and was able to get firsthand classroom experience in her chosen field. Another gifted athlete taught gymnastics after school to small children for the city's recreation department.

Of course many students did the traditional service jobs such as making cappuccinos or serving pizza, but we did not underestimate the importance of these jobs. Getting to work on time, dressing properly, and budgeting their earnings were invaluable life lessons appropriate for their age.

An apprenticeship program was instigated but did not always prove successful. The program was challenged in two ways: (1) students often did menial tasks for no pay, and (2) professional people didn't have the time or the skills to teach high school students. But there were a few successes:

Steve was a smooth talker. He always participated in group discussions with comments that were clever, with an edge of cynicism. His deep desire was to enter politics, perhaps first as a campaign manager and then, "Who knows?" His biting and astute observations of current affairs were delivered with humor and wit.

Steve's habit of cartooning on every scrap of paper in his reach was annoying to some teachers. His homework and assignment papers were inevitably doodled on. As part of the apprenticeship program, we located a famous *MAD* magazine cartoonist who was willing to spend a few hours encouraging Steve. As a result, Steve adopted the use of a sketchpad and began talking about being a political cartoonist. Steve's experience with a professional cartoonist allowed him to see the potential of his wit and artistic talents.

## Ability Grouping

We should never underestimate the impact students have on each other, nor their ability to learn from one another. High school students are keenly aware of the responses and values of their fellow students. When classes have students with mixed intellectual abilities and a variety of socioeconomic backgrounds, students find common ground and make friends with a variety of people.

We maintain that high school students need to learn tolerance for different ethnicities, physical abilities, artistic abilities, and mental abilities. How are students going to learn about people who are different if they are always grouped with people who are the same? In life we are always meeting people with various ethnic, cultural, and intellectual backgrounds. By mixing ability groupings in school we learn tolerance. We learn what the common denominator is between people and where there is common ground.

While special education certainly has its important place in the realm of high school education, it has become a way of life for increasing numbers of students. In fact, special education classes have become a catchall for a wide variety of learning, attention, and behavior anomalies. Once admitted to these programs students find it hard to rejoin their regular classes, as they fall further behind and begin to experience symptoms of alienation and withdrawal. They may also suffer from the stigma of being labeled "slow" or, worse, "retarded." Here's an example of how a "special education" student benefited from being placed in classes with mixed abilities:

Neil was a big handsome kid who could tear down an engine, put it back together, and have it running better. His pleasure reading consisted of hot rod magazines and automobile traders. Neil obviously possessed many talents, but writing was not one of them. Neil's inability to learn how to write had landed him in special education classes from elementary school until the tenth grade—when he transferred to our school. He told us that in eighth grade they had given him a worksheet and a green crayon and told him to color in the picture of a frog.

By the time he found his way to our school Neil was thoroughly disheartened and had such a low opinion of himself that he just sat in class without speaking to anyone. He had been under tremendous pressure to learn to write. The focus of his education had been on his shortcomings, not on his strengths.

We set out to help Neil relax and then gave him alternative ways to demonstrate his learning. It took time, but Neil found ways to shine, especially when the environmental studies class made a video. He handled the camera with great finesse. And at one assembly he made an impassioned anti-smoking speech to "his friends and fellow students." Neil had a sly sense of humor and became popular with the girls.

As his English teacher, Ellen was challenged by his inability to write, but she looked for other ways for him to respond to the literature. One day out of the blue, he wrote a three-line poem called "Don't Eat Yellow Snow," which somehow struck the funny bone of the class and they were all in tears of laughter. Ellen had tears as well, for those were the first words she had seen Neil write in the first year he was at our school.

Neil decided to stay in high school an extra year, but he did graduate with his friends. Just because he couldn't write didn't mean he couldn't learn.

Being enrolled in classes with mixed abilities and skill levels helped Neil regain his confidence and he began to feel better about himself. During his senior year he attended the Environmental Earth Summit in Brazil as a student representative from our school. He came back glowing with a sense of accomplishment.

At Mountain View High School we not only didn't segregate "slow" learners from everyone else, we also didn't restrict the classes to particular grade levels. This not only helped eliminate the separation and rivalries that age and grade groupings invariably create, it also improved the academic environment. We must stress, however, that the only way mixing widely varying academic abilities within the same class can work is in small classes of eight to twelve students. This enables teachers to provide individual instruction when needed.

There were many wonderful moments in our classes when our accelerated learners were teaming up with students with less developed skills in linguistic or mathematical areas of study. These occasions demonstrated the efficacy of colearning and peer mentoring when the students worked together to solve a problem or complete a class project. These occasions also worked to keep the students with deficiencies in certain areas of comprehension from being viewed as somehow different or "special." Instead of focusing on the deficiencies or weaknesses in their ability to learn, we concentrated on the strengths all the students shared.

When the curriculum is not so heavily weighted toward rote memorization and the recitation of facts, but uses a more active and experiential approach to learning, even a so-called special education student can participate right along with everyone else. When students with different ways of learning are assigned to work on a project together, they naturally help each other and a learning exchange takes place.

For example, a student who may be weak in linguistic skills and strong in spatial intelligence could be paired with a strong linguistic learner on a mapping project. While identifying the original place names of local indigenous people on this map, the two students could learn from each other and strengthen their skills. The spatial learner who is good at making maps but less skilled with the indigenous names and their spellings can learn from the linguistically skilled student how to correctly spell and pronounce these place names. The linguistic learner can pick up tips about map making and a sense of direction from the spatial learner.

In our estimation, it is good for brighter teens to be placed in classes with teens who struggle. How are we to have a kinder and gentler world without compassion for each other? Here's an example of how a "gifted" student benefited from our program:

Susan originally transferred into our school because she said that she was so busy every minute of the day with her advanced placement classes that she had no time for music practice and for the environmental work she was committed to.

Susan graduated with the highest SAT scores ever at our school, scores that guaranteed a place for her in any university. We expected that she would go right into one of the biggies and continue her academic career. But she took a year off to travel with a performance troupe who presented an environmental program for high school students. That accomplished, she entered a midsized university that offered an exceptional program in environmental science.

In her somewhat shy and unassuming way, Susan was a brilliant organizer of student activities, but above all she inspired us all with her concern for her fellow students and the environment. We believe Susan benefited by being in a mixed-ability grouping and so did she.

## Altruistic Activities

We strongly believed in social responsibility at our school and continually sought ways to get our students involved in projects and efforts in which they could contribute to the community at large. We required each student to perform ten hours per semester of some kind of community service, and arranged ways for them to work in groups to earn these credits.

One such effort was an "adopt a beach" program run by a neighboring city. Once a month the entire school participated in picking up litter at one of the public beach parks that many of them frequented on the weekends. Our school's name was placed on a small sign at the entrance to the beach indicating our efforts to keep it clean. Other group projects included preparing dinners for the homeless who frequented the winter shelter operated by the churches in our community. The students also collected pledges and joined an AIDS walk.

Our community service coordinator arranged for students to volunteer at the local hospital while others put in hours at the local veterinary clinic and with the Humane Society. Still others worked a few hours each week at a nursery school. This community service program

introduced students to the rewards of altruism and for some it provided a glimpse of a possible career in community service. And sometimes the community service they performed turned into a lifeline of
stability:

Lacey was living with her mother when she enrolled in our school. She was
one of many students we've encountered over the years who'd had a fairly
stable and supportive family life until her parents suddenly split up. Lacey
divided her time between both parents' homes, but then her father left the
area and her mother took on a full-time job. By tenth grade Lacey was left
mostly on her own.

At school she often talked about the good times when her parents were
still together. She'd owned a horse and spent all of her spare time riding and
caring for it. But with the divorce settlement the horse had to be sold and
Lacey felt as if she'd lost not only her stable family life but also her best friend.

For her community service project Lacey chose a horse rescue program
run by the Humane Society. She quickly made friends with the other vol-
unteers and was soon devoting extra hours caring for the neglected horses.
The experience helped her move beyond her own feeling of abandonment
and resulted in improved attentiveness at school.

## Encouraging Students to Take College Classes

The transition from high school to college is difficult for many
students. One of our graduates came back for a visit after her first
semester away at a university. She was amazed at how impersonal the
classes were. "No one knows whether you are there or not," she
lamented. She said she missed the familiarity of her hometown and
was shocked at the impersonal nature of the university campus environment.

We encouraged the college-bound students to get a taste of college before they left high school by concurrent enrollment in a community college. The local community college offered a program in
which high school students could take up to two classes in any given
semester:

Michelle was a straight-A student. Her expressionless cute face belied her
silly sense of humor. When she broke into one of her rare big smiles, she lit
up the room. Math was her forte and she received accelerated lessons in our
personalized classes. But by twelfth grade she had left high school math in
the dust.

We encouraged her to enroll in an evening advanced calculus class at the
community college. Her father, who was an accountant, enrolled in the class

as well. This was a unique father-daughter activity, which they enjoyed together. Not only were Michelle's academic needs met, but she was able to experience the college campus and preview the independence it would afford her. The personal attention of the high school was gone, but she had her father to help her with transportation and any tough challenges in calculus. She received both high school and college credit for this class.

Other students took photography classes, specialized science such as oceanography, or foreign languages that were not available at our school. This option increased the enrichment level for our students and gave them experience that would make their transition to a college campus much easier in the future.

## TWENTY QUESTIONS FOR PARENTS

1. Does your teenager complain that the subjects he or she is studying are not relevant to his or her life?

2. Does your teenager understand that the high school curriculum is the vehicle through which culture is transmitted to him or her?

3. Do you know if the subjects taught to your student are the ones that are needed to prepare for the desired future? How are the subjects determined?

4. In this information age, is solely the acquisition of information a desirable goal or are there other goals in your child's education?

5. Do you pressure your teenager for high scores on the standardized tests?

6. Is the curriculum at your high school driven by standardized test scores? Do you feel it is missing something?

7. Is your student dependent on test scores for self-esteem or does he or she feel defeated by low test scores?

8. Does your school district include input from parents when making curriculum choices? Should it?

9. Has your teenager had eyesight and hearing checked? Is he or she getting adequate sleep and eating nutritional meals?

10. Are you aware of your child's learning style and how it might be effected by the teaching style of the school?

11. Is your teenager being channeled into a specialized school that focuses on a single subject such as science, computers, or art? Is this what your teenager wants for him- or herself? Is it what you want for your teenager?

12. Does the high school your teenager is attending have students interact with the community or is the school kept separate from the neighborhood?

13. Is your teenager engaged in an apprenticeship, work experience, or community college classes?

14. Would your teenager rather be "doing something" than listening to a lecture?

15. Do you encourage your teenager to begin to take an active role in life by expressing political, moral, or philosophic opinions at home? Does this happen in school?

16. Is your student on an academic track in which he or she is grouped with other students with the same ability? Do you agree with this system of grouping by ability?

17. Do you believe your child would benefit by being in a class with learners who are more accelerated as well as those who are struggling?

18. Does your school teach anything about helping those less fortunate through any kind of community service?

19. Does the curriculum at your high school teach the subjects that you value for your child?

20. Is your child engaged in a challenging and satisfying course of study?

## CHAPTER FIVE

# Teachers Are the Ticket

Ellen was in her mid-twenties when she stood in front of a classroom of teenagers for the first time. On that fateful first day she recalled having been a teenager herself and wishing that her high school classes had been fun instead of boring. As a new teacher she wanted to be friends with her students. They were going to enjoy this class together. She couldn't wait to get started.

The nightmare began right there on that very first day. When Ellen turned to write her name on the board, the students threw spit-wads at her. She was called to the office for a five-minute errand and when she returned they had locked her out of the classroom. One handsome athlete sat in the back of the class flirting with her by lifting his shirt up and exposing his bare chest. They didn't laugh at her jokes and didn't turn in their homework. Why did this happen? She was supposed to be their cool teacher.

Out of desperation, Ellen sought the advice of a seasoned teacher. She chuckled at the antics of the students and let Ellen know that teenagers want an adult as a teacher, not someone who acts like their peer. She was sorry to inform her but Ellen had lost the class that semester and try as she might she would not get them back.

Her advice was that next time Ellen should come to the classroom with the authority of an adult, a person who had some expertise to impart. She should also make academic demands that challenged the students to fulfill class requirements to earn a grade. She should clearly define the boundaries for their behavior and the consequences of going beyond those boundaries. Then she could develop friendships if the students were so inclined. The teenagers in their characteristic way were just demanding that we come into right relationship as student/ teacher, then they would cooperate.

Good teachers are the key to good education. But what makes a good teacher: credentials, good training, teaching experience? Teachers are judged by their knowledge of the subject matter, their ability to teach it, and the standardized test scores of the students in their classes. Our experience confirms that the first two of these three attributes are essential, but another is equally important. Teachers should truly care about the students and have compassion for them. This last attribute of compassion is problematic with teenagers. Teens are making the passage to adulthood, which entails scrutinizing the adults around them. They are challenging everything that adults are telling them and often challenge the integrity of the adults themselves.

Former middle school teacher Theresa Bulla-Richards puts it this way:

Adolescents tend to be quite challenging in that they question your paradigm. They challenge your worldview; they challenge everything from the way you dress to what you are doing with your life; and they wonder why you aren't living up to what you claim to be your ideals. I see that as the adolescent's job. They are here to remind us of our hypocrisy. But because of that they are resented.

You can't be with them and also hold onto many guises—they see right through you and you can't be with them and maintain your defenses. . . . That energy is also for the world—to transform society . . . to see what needs to be changed and help it to happen.

Teens are desperately searching for adults they can look up to, and at the same time knocking the pedestal out from under anyone who gets too high and mighty. Many who have tried working with teens decry the lack of respect. But if your love for them can withstand their challenges, you earn their respect.

Teens can be difficult and troublesome because many of them are going through huge challenges and trying times. If prospective teachers don't have an affinity for teenagers they shouldn't be high school teachers. Just as they shouldn't baby-sit for toddlers if they can't stand changing diapers. A teenager comes with challenges that can't be avoided, but can be overcome with compassion.

## WHAT MAKES A GOOD TEACHER GOOD?

For decades the education reforms have rolled on with little overall improvement. Calls have been made for more structure, less structure, more accountability, less interference by government, sticking to the basics, more diversity training, on and on. Education experts seem finally to have settled on the idea that the quality of the teachers is central to good education. We agree. In this section we will look at what makes a good teacher good, although measuring teacher performance is very subjective, as we shall see in the following examples:

Steve conducted quiet, thoughtful math classes. He carefully and incrementally presented a new type of problem and how to solve it. As the students worked independently, he made his way around the classroom, immersing himself in each student's effort. His empathy for the struggle of the student was shown in his patient and to-the-point explanations. No one seemed to be in a hurry in his classroom and yet everyone was engaged. As the daily lesson was grasped, they returned to an individualized program of study he had formulated for each student's strengths and weaknesses. The students raved about how much they learned from Steve.

You could hear Larry's resonant voice through the walls of his classroom. He paced as he taught history, stopping to put bulleted points on the blackboard. Students were brought to the front of the class to perform or "role-play" historical events. His own occasional zany antics encouraged students to cut loose with their playful interpretations.

His passion aroused the students to indignation over political injustice. Often the class took on huge issues as their own, writing letters to the local newspaper editor and even to the president of the United States. He approached the students as agents of change, as he brought them with him mentally on an enjoyable and fearsome romp through history. Students raved about how much they learned from Larry.

How do we measure these teachers? By mastery of subject matter, by performance, by student learning, or by the example they set for youth? We cannot overlook that mild, empathetic Steve and roaring, animated Larry both taught from the heart with tremendous compassion for their students.

Four themes emerge when defining effective teachers:

1. Knowledge and love of the subject matter
2. Verbal skills and love of conversation
3. Experience with teenagers and a love for them that is empathetic but not indulgent
4. Personal integrity and strength to direct a class, hold the line, and balance freedom in the classroom with responsibility

## Teaching What You Love

If you remember the teachers who made an impression on you, they were probably the ones who loved the material they taught, whether it was Shakespeare or the Pythagorean theorem. To inspire enthusiasm and infuse a subject with life, a teacher has to love it. Passion for a subject comes from interest and familiarity with it.

In high schools most teachers are teaching in their field, yet every year one in three teachers is asked to teach a class a day for which he or she has not been trained. The absolute bottom line for teachers is that they know the subject matter and be enthusiastic about it. In this way they can pursue what they love and share it with their students.

We grow as teachers when we are active, passionate learners in our field. Teachers working in their area of passion bring in current events, share recently read books with their students, and take their classes on field trips to exhibits and events relating to their subject. Teachers need to be given latitude to innovate, design, and initiate learning activities. Nothing is as dry as a tired lecture written years ago with no current updates.

In the 1980s we saw bumper stickers telling us to "Follow Your Bliss" and "Do Your Dream." While these messages might seem a bit self-indulgent, the idea they convey certainly applies to teaching. We shouldn't enter a profession that we don't have a deep love for. Prospective teachers should try to steer their career toward the subjects for which they have a true affinity:

When Larry became a high school teacher, he really wanted to teach English. He'd been a lifelong reader and lover of literature and longed to share his enthusiasm with his students. He held an interdisciplinary degree in English, history, and political science and eagerly agreed to teach freshman English when the opportunity presented itself.

But right away Larry realized that his teaching style was not well suited for the serious study of grammar and composition. He preferred a very active classroom with lots of hands-on activities and role playing. And he quickly found in the English class that his style and energy were not well suited for discussing and interpreting literature. After a few painful false starts and many anxious moments worrying that the class was a failure, Larry ended up turning it into a creative writing workshop. The students finished the year writing stories and designing and publishing a creative writing magazine.

In contrast to his experience with the English class, Larry's civics and American history classes always felt to him like unqualified successes. His energy and enthusiasm for history and politics were easily transferable to various hands-on activities. He never spent much time conducting intimate discussions in those classes, but had his students up and about role playing, conducting surveys, and taking an active interest in local politics.

## Teachers as Storytellers, Communicators, and Listeners

The only consistent "tested for" indicator of what makes a good teacher good is high verbal skills. New York and Connecticut, among other states, are looking for performance and passion in their teachers and now require videotapes showing aspiring teachers interacting with students. We think performance is what a teacher is actually doing in a classroom, but performance has been routinely overlooked in preparing teachers for the classroom.

Teachers need more training in how to guide group discussions and how to maintain student interest through storytelling and active listening. Storytelling is largely overlooked as a teaching method and yet it is one of our oldest forms of communication. Far from being lost to us as a technique, storytelling is an art that can be learned.

In traditional societies the storyteller was the teacher. The storyteller recorded the history of the group and passed on the tales that defined the mores and values of the culture. Tales not only entertained and delighted the listeners but taught the valuable lessons that maintained the group. Favorites were told and retold, and a good story stays with you long after the final words have been spoken.

This ancient art form is cocreative and interactive. Listeners have to fill in the visual details in their minds with personal interpretation. The teller adjusts the story to the nonverbal feedback from the listeners. Any good storyteller will confide that the story changes for each audience. What is the value of the story?

1. A story is remembered.
2. A story can transfer important cultural, moral, and sociological information.
3. A story can give examples of ideas in practice. Listeners learn to apply metaphors to real life.
4. A story can convey levels of meaning, emotional as well as intellectual.
5. Personal stories can show students that teachers make mistakes and face challenges too.
6. Storytelling is contagious—listeners become tellers.

Teaching is not just passing out information from the teacher to the student. It is development of the mind and heart and the passing on of the culture. To be a teacher is like being a guide along the path of knowledge, trying to take the students with you, using provocative questions to keep them from going down a dead end.

Telling the story is not a frivolous pursuit. A good storyteller must know the story and have intimate knowledge of the subject. With this knowledge the storyteller captivates the listener and brings him or her along on the path to understanding. Like any good conversation, a story is an exchange of energy.

## Experience with and Love of Teenagers

It's impossible to judge what today's teenagers are like by trying to recall your own life as a teenager. Prospective teachers should be provided with opportunities to work with teens in a variety of capacities in order to acquire the skills needed to be successful leaders in the classroom. There is no better way to learn how to relate to teens than by working with them in a context outside the classroom.

For ten years before Richard became a teacher he worked with teenagers through various programs administered by the U.S. Forest Service. This experience gave him firsthand knowledge of how eager teens are to learn new skills and to do a good job. In his capacity as supervisor of teenagers and young adults in activities ranging from fighting forest fires to maintenance and construction, he obtained a sense of how to show respect for them while letting them know what was expected of them in return. He learned to be patient with them when they were experiencing some kind of personal crisis and he also learned that providing a regular routine of work and responsibility tempered by "down time" helped them gain confidence to face each personal crisis and overcome it.

This priceless experience enabled Richard to relax and be confident the first time he stepped into a high school classroom as a teacher. The lessons learned in the Forest Service were directly transferable to his new profession. From his years of experience he knew when to be casual and relaxed or formal and stern. he knew when to let teens have their way and when to call their bluff.

Because Richard knew what teens were capable of accomplishing and had learned how to motivate them without coming on too strong, his relationships with his students were based on real-world experiences rather than on what someone else said. It was his immersion with teens that gave him confidence to teach them.

There are various ways for prospective teachers to gain experience with teenagers. Church groups, summer camps, and the YMCA/YWCA are just a few of the avenues available to gain this experience. Taking the time to find out what working with teenagers is really like can help prospective teachers discover if they're really cut out for the job.

## Personal Integrity and Strength

It is difficult for a teacher to exemplify leadership qualities and integrity in the classroom if he or she lacks those qualities. Over the years we witnessed teachers who hadn't achieved a level of leadership or personal integrity that enabled them to successfully manage a classroom. Examples of this included teachers who tried too hard to make teens like them by talking about their own experimentation with drugs, teachers who chummed up to students and identified the administration as the common enemy, and teachers who favored an elite group of students over the rest of the class.

As teachers we are not trying to win over our students by creating the impression that we suffer under the same pressures they do. Teens aren't looking for an adult to commiserate with. They are looking for hope and inspiration and dignity. Teachers must hold themselves up as examples of integrity in order to provide the classroom structure in which students can thrive. Students will be free to express themselves only when they feel they are in safe hands. They want teachers who can maintain control while at the same time allowing creativity to flourish. Teens will push the limits in a classroom until they find the boundaries and then they will relax and get to work. Teachers need to set those boundaries and maintain them in a fair way, not by sharing stories of when they did things that lacked integrity but by becoming an example of integrity and strength.

## Qualities That Can't Be Measured

A good teacher knows how to modulate the energy in a classroom and possesses an intuitive feeling for where the class is at any given moment and where they need to go. Teachers should be able to read the mood of their students and know what is best in any given situation. If the particular lesson has gone stale, the teacher needs to be free to take the class for a walk or on a short field trip, or simply tell a story.

Keeping the learning atmosphere alive in a classroom sometimes calls for a radical departure from the planned curriculum. Good teachers can sense when the energy gets bogged down and they need the freedom to do something about it. Qualities of the heart can't be measured but are immediately recognizable when we enter the classroom. We can see when a teacher has faith in students; he or she is not cynical or demeaning. These qualities of the heart are amply rewarded.

One student at our school surprised his English teacher and the other students by enthusiastically thanking her for a great class. A few other students added, "Yeah, thanks." As this student's enthusiasm for the class grew, every day seemed to generate a heartfelt "thank you." Other teachers reported that the "thank yous" were moving through the school. They were entirely unsolicited and warmly welcomed.

Many of the students who attended our small high school have stayed in touch with us by e-mail, phone calls, and letters. We hear from them as they travel to places we talked about in our classes, when they graduate from college, or when they have children. Sometimes they just drop by to say hello.

## Master Teachers

A master teacher has high expectations for every student. A combination of focused intellectual "press" and personal support characterizes these dedicated teachers. Effective teachers can approach a topic from several points of view and are always on the lookout for materials that augment the subject, such as videos, music, magazine articles, art, and experts in the field who are willing to come to class.

Here's what master teacher Eliot Wigginton has to say about effective teaching in his book *Sometimes a Shining Moment: The Foxfire Experience—Twenty Years Teaching in a High School Classroom*:

Teaching basic skills and life survival skills, showing how the world works, fostering involvement in and appreciation for the arts, building personal traits such as curiosity, self-confidence, independence, and self-esteem, and simultaneously moving the student beyond self into a caring relationship with humanity and the environment and a sense of the interdependence of all life—a big job indeed . . . the job of everyone from whom young people gain knowledge. It is for this reason that the best teachers, realizing the limitations on their time and energy, make sure that all the projects and lessons that take place in their classes serve double and triple functions; and they constantly strive to find activities that are so compelling and so rich that they go even beyond that. They are, in short, activities that serve nearly all the goals simultaneously, with no real increase in the time and energy required. . . . Suddenly rather than being narrow and pinched, they see things whole.

## TEACHING AS IT SHOULD BE

In all the current discussions about raising teaching standards and holding schools accountable for how well students perform on standardized tests, one vital topic is missing: the human side. How can we be effective teachers if we can't claim some kind of friendship with our students? If learning really takes place within the context of relationships, what relationships are appropriate between teachers and students? If we don't feel a calling to teach or aren't allowed to do what we do best in the classroom, how will our students ever learn anything? This section looks at the aspects of teaching that are often ignored but that actually form the framework for a successful experience in the classroom.

### Friendship

Each day when Richard arrived at school he made a special point of greeting all the students he encountered. Our school had a long open-air walkway that led to the office and it was lined with benches where the students gathered in the morning while waiting for classes to begin. Every morning Richard greeted each of the students along the row of benches, calling them by name and asking how they were doing.

Occasionally he sat down with one or two of them and engaged them in a conversation. The subject of these talks was usually trivial but his effort made a big difference in the way the students related to him. They talked about surfing, skateboarding, a recent movie, or what they did over the weekend. These contacts broke down the barriers that seemed to separate teacher from student and helped establish a connection that was strengthened as the year progressed.

Addressing each student by name resulted in a mutual feeling of friendliness and acceptance. One of the students even told Richard that her mood was lifted when he greeted her and offered her a smile every morning. She said she often came to school feeling glum and looked forward to the greeting to cheer her up. This simple practice helped maintain close contact and open communication with Richard's students. The effort was repaid many times over with a sense of community that was always present at the school.

Teachers can be much more effective if they can connect with each student in an individual way. This can be accomplished by finding common ground with students and pursuing communication with them on that level. Richard was able to do this most readily through talking about sports, the arts, or entertainment. Relating to students through an activity that they love helps them see the teacher as a human, not just some authority figure in a coat and tie.

Richard found that talking to the teenage boys about sports activities like surfing and actually going surfing with them when the opportunity presented itself opened the doors for communication to flow and friendships to develop. Establishing a relationship based on interests and activities outside the classroom helps students develop a genuine liking for their teachers and a greater desire to learn from them:

Jim was a typically active ninth grader who would have rather been out skateboarding or surfing than in the classroom. He'd been diagnosed with some attention deficit and reading difficulties and hadn't done well in the public schools. Jim's parents felt that he needed more individual attention, so they enrolled him at our school.

But Jim didn't seem to integrate well at Mountain View. He was constantly challenging the authority of the teachers, ditching classes, and causing trouble in the surrounding neighborhood. His parents were determined to keep Jim enrolled in spite of the conferences, letters home, and suspensions.

As a tenth grader Jim ended up in Richard's Friday morning ceramics class and they weren't on very good terms because of all the discipline issues that Richard had addressed with him in his role as an administrator. But they got to know each other because the ceramics class was a more casual workshop atmosphere and one day Richard asked Jim if he wanted to go surfing after class.

Jim eagerly agreed, so they drove to his house and picked up his board, then headed up the coast to a popular surfing beach. This routine became a regular part of the Friday afternoon activities and Richard eventually created an official surfing class that grew to include half a dozen other students.

But that first day out with Jim was special because it completely redefined the student-teacher relationship. The roles of "bad boy" and "hard guy" were dropped. They re-created their relationship based on our mutual love of

surfing. They began communicating on a level of appreciation and understanding and this resulted in an easing of the tension surrounding Jim's previous behavior at school.

As Jim got to know Richard and trust him, Jim actually began making
an effort to improve in school and stay out of trouble. That's not to say that
he became a perfect angel. He still tested the boundaries and pushed the
limits, but the anger and resentment that he'd previously exhibited at school
evaporated. Jim graduated and went into the trades, becoming a very competent heavy equipment operator.

In order to establish an open and friendly relationship with her students on the first day of school, Ellen put her home phone number
on the board and said, "Please call me if you are having trouble with
an assignment or anything you don't understand." This informality
and openness surprised some of the kids. When the calls started to
come in at the beginning of the year, the students were reticent on
the phone but gradually gained confidence and usually called when
they really needed help.

She was glad to be able to help because the next class session
would not have a student who was tuned out because he or she was
lost. It saved time and often students might call and talk one-on-
one if they were reluctant to let the whole class know they didn't
understand.

## Relationship

We believe that it is the relationship with the teacher that draws out
the inherent intelligence of a student. In that relationship, the student
often remembers who he or she is and awakens to his or her inner light
because the teacher sees that light and acknowledges it, drawing it
forth.

John O'Donohue's book *Anam Cara, A Book of Celtic Wisdom*
provided this poetic inspiration for Ellen when she was striving to
understand why relationships in teaching are so important:

According to Celtic spiritual tradition, the soul shines all around the body
like a luminous cloud. When you are very open—appreciative and trusting—
with another person, your two souls flow together. This deeply felt bond with
another person means you have found an *anam cara*, or a "soul friend." Your
*anam cara* always beholds your light and beauty, and accepts you for who
you truly are.

In Celtic spirituality, the *anam cara* friendship awakens the fullness and mystery of your life. You are joined in an ancient and eternal union with humanity that cuts across all barriers of time, convention, philosophy, and definition. When you are blessed with an *anam cara*, the Irish believe you have arrived at the most sacred place: home.

This kind of relationship is entirely possible between a student and a teacher. By example a teacher can inspire a student to live a daily life of excellence. By expressing compassion and affectionate interest in the student, a teacher can draw out the idealism and humanity of that student:

Amy was a twin whose sister was outgoing and popular. Amy was thin with long dark hair and bangs that often covered her face and was so shy that she had been home schooled for several years. Her mother had convinced her to give our school a try because it was a safe, friendly place.

Amy would write teachers little folded-up notes explaining the reasons for not completing her homework. Once she wrote that she had thought about the subject for several hours and couldn't decide what to write. The staff was encouraging and patient as we discussed Amy's progress in our staff meetings.

Gradually Amy developed a relationship of trust with Carol, the art teacher, who was also thin with long hair and bangs, only Carol's hair was gray. We were all delighted to see Amy and Carol laughing and talking together in the art room. They truly enjoyed each other's company. Amy began to produce extraordinary artwork. With Carol's encouragement, support, and friendship, Amy's skillful artistry took on a unique beauty.

As Amy's confidence grew, she began to complete her assignments in other classes. The staff was astonished to discover the capabilities and depth of her understanding. Carol's authentic and soulful friendship had drawn out Amy's inherent intelligence.

For a relationship to be productive and mutual, it must be built in an environment where both teacher and student want to be there. We always insisted that it be a student's desire to enroll at our school. Where appropriate we designed curriculums that included self-observation and asked students to reflect upon their relationship to their teacher, parents, and the rest of the class. High school students often don't realize the importance of the relationships they are developing unless they are asked to reflect upon them.

## A Vocation

Let's suppose for a minute that we could go outside the confines of the current educational system to locate good teachers. Let's suppose we weren't required to hire people with teaching credentials, but could go out to the community at large and locate the best teachers. What kind of criteria would guide our choices?

The Indian philosopher Jiddu Krishnamurti had this to say about what makes a good teacher from his book *Education and the Significance of Life*:

People who have no academic degrees often make the best teachers because they are willing to experiment; not being specialists, they are interested in learning, in understanding life. For the true teacher, teaching is not a technique; it is his way of life; like a great artist he would rather starve than give up his creative work. Unless one has this burning desire to teach, one should not be a teacher. It is of the utmost importance that one discover for oneself whether one has this gift, and not merely drift into teaching because it is a means of livelihood. (p. 109)

Krishnamurti believed that an educator is not merely a giver of information, but someone who points the way to wisdom and truth. He believed that educators must try to help their students discover the truth behind problems without projecting on students their own idiosyncrasies and habits of thought. One of the most important qualities of a teacher according to Krishnamurti is the possession of self-awareness. He called upon teachers to examine the relationship of the individual to society. He also stressed the importance for teachers to have great understanding and the strength of patience and love.

Education is obviously more than merely the assimilation of information. In order to truly educate our children we need to teach them how to look beyond the facts, how to comprehend their relationship to the world, and how to engage in it in a productive way. In our great rush to train specialists able to operate in a compartmentalized society we have forgotten to teach the appropriate responses to the complex interrelationships of life. We've forgotten to point out to our students the connections that need to be maintained in order to promote a harmonious and healthy society.

Teachers should be able to set their own fears and prejudices aside and help their students acquire the skills of inquiry. As Krishnamurti says, a good teacher will encourage his or her students to investigate individual and social values and develop an integrated intelligence and comprehension of life that can identify the true value of all things and flower in love and goodness.

So where do we find these wonderful and wise teachers? When reading Krishnamurti's definition we might envision the perfect teacher to be a wizened old philosopher like Socrates, whose goal was to awaken the spirit of self-inquiry in his students. Is it realistic to believe we can find people willing to enter the teaching profession who have a true love for the vocation, who long to guide students to the realization of their own true potential? Does anyone really care enough about young people to be willing to subject themselves to low pay, long hours, and hazardous duty? The answer is yes:

Jim Sargent is a high school teacher from Ventura, California, who gave up a profitable partnership in an insurance firm to pursue his love of teaching. Sargent talked the administrators at his school into letting him set up a small history class for "underachievers." He scoured the campus for students who were pretty much uninterested in school but whom he felt had the potential to be strong leaders. Having grown up in a working-class town where "the only educated people were teachers," Sargent wanted to help students who were growing up in similar circumstances to have a better chance to graduate and enroll in college. His classes are hands-on, with plenty of role playing and looking at real-world issues like local politics and the education system.

In Jim Sargent and many other truly inspired teachers we find some common qualities: caring, empathy, and compassion for their students. Sargent's goal was to help students from the long-ignored working class of society, those disenfranchised from power, to have an equal chance at success. He structured his classes to appeal to them, offering them a chance to be the standouts in the class without having to compete with the traditional "high achievers" from more privileged backgrounds. His formula has worked and is resulting in students getting turned onto learning. With every lesson he asks each student to participate. One of Sargent's students said, "Being able to say what I want is easier to do now. I don't care what people think. I just raise my hand and say it."

## The Latitude to Do Their Best

It is very beneficial for students when teachers are allowed to do what they do best. Over the years we hired a number of teachers who possessed a particular expertise and we encouraged them to use that skill in the classroom. One of our English teachers had many years of experience working in prep schools and had also graduated from one of the top prep schools in the nation. He brought to our school a much more rigorous approach to academics than our students were used to. He liked to put a full academic "press" on his students and often required them to rewrite papers several times until they "got it right."

Instead of telling him that his approach really didn't fit the style of our school and requesting that he change his approach to match what we were doing, we encouraged him to pursue it. If just so happened that we had several students who really wanted to be challenged academically. They thrived in his classes and said that their high school education had been greatly broadened by this teacher and his rigorous approach.

Another teacher began working for us in our math program and had a special way of communicating with teenagers that showed a great deal of understanding and empathy. Even though he was highly skilled as a math teacher, his degree was in philosophy, so when he expressed a desire to teach a philosophy class we gave him the go-ahead.

After the new class had been under way for a while it was easy to see that his real love was facilitating philosophical discussions. He selected the book *Sophie's World* as the text for the class and led his students through an analysis of the world's philosophical traditions. His philosophy class added great depth to our curriculum and inspired students to read about and explore more deeply the underlying themes and archetypes of world culture.

## THE CHALLENGE

When Ellen read that the National Education Association was offering teachers "homicide insurance," she wondered again why anyone would choose the teaching profession. The nation's largest teachers union is offering a $150,000 benefit for the families of members slain on the job.

Besides the much publicized safety issue, which was addressed in Chapter 1, teachers face a number of real daily challenges that interfere with their ability to guide their students. The dynamics inside the classroom are dramatically different from what most parents remember from their school days. This section elucidates some of the challenges faced by teachers.

## Classroom Size

In deciding what high school is best for a student, the single most significant thing to consider is class size. A class jam-packed with adolescent energy is too much for most teachers to handle. Large classes kill creativity and make crowd control a nightmare. No teacher can develop a relationship with a student in a crowded classroom.

Traditional high school teachers face as many as 150 to 170 students a day. These teachers are lucky to know the names of all their students before the end of the first semester. Developing more than cursory relationships with individual students is nearly impossible due to the sheer numbers.

Even though positive teacher/student relationships have been identified as a crucial aspect of a good education, today's behemoth schools make this difficult at best. School administrators aren't likely to stress the importance of developing positive relationships, which are really only possible in small classes, when the funding for their school is based on maintaining high numbers of students.

In small classes teachers can better know their students, allowing them to identify individual talents and needs. The process of education in a class with fifteen or fewer students also becomes more personalized for the student and therefore more relevant. Engaging in the give and take of discussions directly with the teacher and receiving verbal feedback help students develop a variety of skills and build self-assurance and confidence. Teenagers agree that the best way to improve schools is to reduce class size, according to a 2001 survey *State of Our Nation's Youth*, published by the Horatio Alger Association, www.horatioalger.com.

If you recall the teachers you really admired and learned from, more than likely they were teachers you were able to form some kind of relationship with. Teachers offer more to their students than how to construct a paragraph or balance an equation. When given the opportunity in an intimate classroom setting, good teachers offer their students a part of themselves. They serve as role models and are inspiring and engaging. Students want to learn from teachers like these, but will they get a chance if they are competing for attention with thirty-five or forty other students?

## Mandatory Standardized Curriculum

We feel that the curriculum guidelines set forth by each state are essentially sound for establishing a school curriculum, but they should not be an ironclad mandate. Students will learn more from a teacher who is passionate about the subject he or she is teaching than from a teacher who is forced to follow a curriculum he or she had no part of creating. Each teacher has unique interests and academic strengths. How can we standardize the teaching of millions of unique individuals and the learning of millions of unique students? What are we trying to accomplish? Will a standardized curriculum turn the teacher in the following story into standardized and boring "rule-book" teacher?

One colorful and gifted English teacher, Mrs. LaFarge, was very dramatic in her presentation of literature. It was no wonder as she'd been an active participant in amateur theater in the community. She thrived in the roomful of outspoken and fresh minds and could make the suspense, the intrigue, the romance, and the adventure of literature come alive for her students. Her ability to foster a love for literature was phenomenal and the work that she drew out of her students was often brilliant. Some of them had never read for pleasure before taking her class. She gave the gift of a lifetime by instilling a passion for literature

But she was not very efficient in returning homework. Her analytical powers left a bit to be desired. Critical thinking was something she could do with effort, but it was not her natural gift. Her grading was inconsistent and she lost track of time, repeatedly keeping her students long after the class period was over.

Like all of us, Mrs. LaFarge had her strengths and weaknesses. Was she a good teacher? Would you want your high school student in her class? A powerful political and educational movement is pushing for a standard curriculum to be taught to all students. Will students be losing out if we insist that Mrs. LaFarge stick to a predetermined curriculum and not get so carried away with literature?

We felt that Mrs. LaFarge was a naturally gifted teacher, perfectly suited for the high school classroom and one of the few teachers who her students will never forget. They will probably never forget what she taught them as well. If a standardized or mandatory curriculum goes into effect, Mrs. LaFarge will be limited in her ability to share her gift and our kids will lose out on a lifetime opportunity.

When teachers are told to teach "only the curriculum and all of the curriculum," we are limiting their creativity and even their ability to impart their unique wisdom. Teachers need the opportunity to invent and reinvent elements of the school's curriculum in response to the following:

- The student's interest and ability, which changes with each class
- The teacher's own learning and development
- The level of passion the teacher feels for the various components of subjects taught

We believe that with fewer directives and more support for the teacher's inventiveness and concern for his or her students, we will keep the best and the brightest in the profession; classes will be lively, students will be inspired, and more will be learned.

Most teachers who feel responsible to cover all of the mandates are engaged in a race against time. And yet additions to the standard curriculum appear regularly. Whenever someone has a solution to the "drug problem" or the "health crisis" or a "safety problem" or the "literacy problem," more directives seem to be heaped upon teachers.

## Standardized Testing

Standardized testing creates tension for teachers to "teach to the test" instead of teaching to the student. It is also punitive because a teacher is judged by the scores of his or her students. All that is measured of his or her teaching ability is what is asked on the test. The teacher's job and the school's funding are at stake if the students receive low scores.

As every teacher can tell you, every class has students with various abilities, cultural heritages, resources, and interests. The dynamics of each class are unique. One year a certain approach works like magic, the next year it's a flop. If a good teacher seizes the moment to respond to a student's continued interest and enthusiasm for learning, he or she will get behind on the mandatory curriculum and the other students may miss out on "the test." Here's an example of how teaching to the test can leave some students in the dust:

Mrs. Rubalcava's son had little interest in school but was suddenly fascinated with the idea of evolution and wanted to explore humanity's prehistoric origins. She immediately went to visit his teacher and explained her joy about her son's sparked enthusiasm for an academic subject. The teacher responded that it was unfortunate that the class was finished with the unit on prehistory. The mother asked if just this once the teacher might extend the subject for a few days, since it was such a landmark for her son. But the teacher insisted that a few days would put her behind in preparation for "the test."

Delving deeper into any subject means shortchanging another subject, as this conscientious teacher knows. She sticks to the mandatory curriculum and her students get good scores on the standardized tests. She may even get rewarded with "merit pay" regardless of whether she's actually appealing to her students' interests.

We believe that if students want to prepare for a certain test, they should be encouraged to do so. To satisfy this desire our high school offered a Scholastic Aptitude Test (SAT) preparation class as an elective. Scores on the SAT are used by many colleges and universities as part of their entrance requirements and influence the acceptance or rejection of a student into their program.

Paul Houston, executive director of the American Association of School Administrators, said in an article written by Alan J. Borsuk and published by *The Milwaukee Journal Sentinel Online*, June 16, 2001, titled "Standardized Assessment Is Changing Education": "We understand why states are moving to high stakes testing. They want a silver bullet to improve public schools. However, there is no one silver bullet. We need comprehensive reforms that include high standards, safe schools, small class sizes, improved compensation to draw out the best people to education, and a curriculum that engages children in the excitement and joy of learning."

A more cynical view in the same article quotes Caroline M. Hoxby, a Harvard economist who has called testing "undoubtedly the school reform with the highest ratio of benefits to costs." She figured that if the amount spent on testing were used for other reforms, such as raising teacher salaries or reducing class size, it would have virtually no impact. By that standard, testing is certainly providing a big bang for the buck.

Finally we'd like to share parts of a letter to the editor from our local paper, the *Ojai Valley News,* April 6, 2001, titled "Teacher's Lament," in which Jeff Madrigal sums up this teacher's challenges very well:

Most of the one hundred or so teachers that I had worked with in seven years and four districts rarely talked of teaching as a life profession until retirement. . . . You see, teaching, or at least the way I teach is a passionate, joyful, sometimes painful search for the truth in each child. At some point in every year the class ceases to be a class and becomes "my kids." Their triumphs and failures become mine.

Parents and policymakers have a difficult time understanding this. They do not see the complexity of the teacher's relationship with "their class."

Policymakers will give us ridiculous incentives and threaten us with consequences based on test scores. They appear unable or unwilling to acknowledge social forces teachers deal with every day in a classroom of thirty-three plus strangers trying to coexist in harmony, positivity and fairness, despite a world that often lacks any trace of these basic human needs. Parents will not acknowledge one of the ten positive experiences for their child, and yet show up one day without warning, and question a teacher's integrity, competence and worthiness to lead the future leaders of the world.

So why do we burn out? Because one day we can't face all of the above with a positive attitude and a sweet smile on our faces. Once this happens, we must leave the profession for the sake of the delicate lives we influence.

After reading this letter, parents shouldn't be surprised to learn from a survey called, "Teacher Turnover, Teacher Shortages, and the Organization of Schools," conducted by Dr. Richard M. Ingersoll, University of Pennsylvania, 2001, that 33 percent of teachers leave the classroom after three years and nearly 50 percent quit after five years.

## THE FUTURE

The future of the teaching profession presents a vastly different landscape from the past. With substantial increases in the numbers of high school students as a result of the "babyboomer echo" and a high rate of teacher attrition, school districts are scrambling to fill in the gap. The dilemma of the looming teacher shortage presents problems and opportunities, while the call to reform the profession has never been louder. The ultimate result will be a radical transformation for both schools and teachers. What we think of as the average teacher may in the future range from someone who began to train for the profession in high school to a midcareer professional or retiree looking to make a meaningful contribution to society. Computers also have a large role to play, as more students are opting to leave school and study at home. Some of the aspects making up what we regard as a new revolution in education are described below.

### A Serious Teacher Shortage

The teaching profession is facing a personnel shortage that is destined to become more acute in the future. While elementary and secondary school enrollment is projected to increase to 53.4 million students nationally through 2005 and grow by 4 percent in public high schools by 2008, according to the National Center for Education Statistics, Projections of Education Statistics to 2012, the average teacher is approaching retirement age. More than half the teachers in the classroom today will be retired six years from now. Fewer people are being attracted to teaching because the salaries are so low and the preparation is becoming more strenuous.

Researchers say that school systems will be scrambling to provide teachers and many already are. The National Teacher Recruitment Clearing House (www.rnt.org) estimates that public schools will need 2.2 million to 2.5 million teachers over the next decade. In 2001 New York was faced with hiring 8,000 new teachers while North Carolina needed to fill 12,000 vacancies.

## Changes in Teacher Education

At a time when there are already too few teachers to fill vacant slots, the mainstream route to becoming a teacher is becoming more difficult. The academic requirements for earning a teaching credential are now more stringent in many states in an effort to raise the quality of education in the classroom. But an unavoidable side effect of these efforts is fewer candidates entering the profession.

Some states have raised the minimum college grade point average requirement for students graduating from credential programs. Others require supervised student teaching (twenty-one states require at least twelve weeks of student teaching prior to completion of teacher preparation program). Some have added more required courses in subjects such as child development, diversity, and educational philosophy, while others require more tests in basic skills. In 2001, thirty-seven states required prospective teachers to pass a basic-skills test, twenty-nine required a subject knowledge test, twenty-four required a subject pedagogy exam, and twenty-three required that all high school teachers must have at least thirty credits or a major in the subject area for which they are licensed.

While these increased requirements may be the best way to improve the academic caliber of persons entering the teaching profession, they are also resulting in fewer trained teachers. Enrollment in teacher colleges is actually decreasing. Capable and interested liberal arts students are avoiding teaching and looking elsewhere.

Although educators across the country are clearly serious about raising the standards for good teaching, they are confronted with an inability to ensure that a qualified adult will be available for every class-room. What are they doing to deal with a teacher shortage that is being driven by the more stringent licensing requirements, the high number of retirees, and the babyboomer echo's push in student numbers?

### New Routes into Teaching

In the future we will see the teaching profession open to more nontraditional candidates. This will be driven by the vast increase in students and the decreasing number of teachers graduating from traditional teacher colleges. Some educators believe that keeping licensing requirements at a bare minimum and allowing school administrators the freedom to hire the people they want will work best to provide more teachers. Proponents of this approach say there is no valid research proving that certified personnel make better teachers. And using fresh recruits without teaching credentials isn't necessarily bad according to a July 2001 article by Marjorie Coeyman from the *Christian Science Monitor* (www.csmonitor.com) titled: "America's Widening Teacher Gap." "We've already discovered in this country that certification is no guarantee of teacher quality," said Kathy Christie, an analyst at the Education Commission of the States in Denver, Colorado. Even today some forty-four states have established alternative routes to teacher certification. Some states such as Mississippi are allowing noneducation majors to teach. A growing number of teachers are teaching out of their field or have never gone to school to become a teacher.

Some of the solutions to the shortage, which is already upon us, have been community colleges offering bachelor's degrees in teacher training or associate degrees in teaching that can be transferred to a university. The cities of Chicago, Los Angeles, and New York are recruiting teachers from overseas. Another common approach being used to expand the number of potential teachers is to attract midcareer professionals into the field. School districts are also luring retirees back to the classroom by allowing them to receive pension benefits while earning a salary.

States are also looking to the high schools to recruit future teachers. North Carolina is offering scholarships to the top four hundred high school graduates who agree upon graduation to teach in one of the state's public schools. Other states are offering college-credit courses to high school students focused on aspects of teaching such as creation of lesson plans, teaching observation, and tutoring younger students. South Carolina has established a high school teacher cadet program that graduated twenty-one thousand students in 1999.

As colleges of education lose their monopoly on teacher preparation, educated people will have several routes into teaching and many adults will spend a few years in the profession. Any college graduate of good character will be eligible to teach. According to Paul T. Hill, coauthor of *Reinventing Public Education,* "Today's shortage of new education school graduates will be permanent. The teaching force will include many educated people who retired from other careers or whose children have left the nest."

## Salaries

Although many states are attempting to raise teacher salaries, progress has been minimal. Teacher unions say that the relative standard of living for their members is at its lowest level in forty years. The salaries are so far behind those of professions with comparable training that a lot of catching up is needed. Impacting on already burdened state budgets, the gains are slow to come.

With entry-level teachers earning $7,500 less than someone starting out in marketing and $15,000 less than a computer scientist, it is easy to understand why college graduates are opting not to pursue teaching. Some states are countering this by increasing the number of scholarships offered to students interested in teaching, increasing the salaries of existing teachers, and giving bonuses to teachers who demonstrate increased knowledge and skill on assessment tests.

Some schools are trying to improve working conditions by upgrading teacher lounges and other amenities. But salary seems to be the bottom line in retaining young teachers. Bonuses for signing teaching contracts can bring $2,000 in Mississippi and $20,000 in Massachusetts. Tax breaks of $250 to $1,500 are also being offered to those willing to enter the profession.

But how far can bonuses and tax breaks go to relieve the real problem? The average salary for a new teacher in the United States was $26,000 in 2001. Let's use the example of a teacher in California with a starting salary of $34,000. After up to five years of college, how does this teacher cover all his or her expenses when rent on an apartment can cost $15,000 a year?

We see a time in the near future when teachers will negotiate salaries. The need for qualified teachers will be so great that the laws of supply and demand will allow them to demand pay commensurate with their experience and training. A school district in Arizona has already implemented a three-tiered system of teacher licensing that includes provisional, professional, and master teacher categories, with pay increases for each tier.

### Computers as Teachers

There is no question that computers will impact the future of education. But we believe that a computer cannot replace a live teacher because of the significance that personal relationships play in learning. According to U.S. Census Bureau figures, the ratio of computers to students in the nation's elementary and secondary schools is one to four. Some experts believe this is the optimum number, according to an article titled "Technology in Teaching," by Lawrence L. Smith, that appeared in *USA Today Magazine*, 1999. In many school districts across the country this model is already a reality. The computer will play its part as an information resource but will not completely replace books or writing by hand.

We see the teachers of the future directing their students to lessons on the computer and spending more time monitoring individual progress. But we feel a teacher's presentation will still be central because students are drawn out by personal interaction. High school students also learn on so many levels within the social environment of a classroom of their peers.

It is clear from statistics that more students than ever are studying at home and are heavily dependent on computers for lessons. But they will need adult supervision and ways to develop friendships with students their own age. Developmentally, teenagers have a need to socialize with peers and relationships with adults they can admire. A complete discussion of the growing home study movement is provided in Chapter 8.

## TWENTY QUESTIONS FOR PARENTS

1. If not all qualified teachers are "good" teachers, then what makes a good teacher good in your estimation?
2. Does your student have good teachers in the school he or she is attending?

3. When you visit and observe a classroom, do you find teachers who love the subject matter, love teenagers, and love conversation?

4. Are the teachers in your child's school given the latitude to innovate? Have you asked the principal about this?

5. Since teachers may be the adult models and mentors for teens, shouldn't they embody personal integrity and leadership? How are these qualities discerned?

6. Do your child's teachers have high expectations for him or her or is your child prejudged by previous grades and reports?

7. Has your teenager developed a friendship with one or more teachers?

8. Do you agree that it is through relationships that learning takes place and that your teenager will benefit by extending relationships beyond the family circle?

9. Does your teenager want to be in the current school environment or is he or she there by coercion?

10. Do you agree with philosopher Krishnamurti that an educator is someone who points the way to wisdom and truth through inquiry?

11. Do you believe that high school teachers can have much of an impact if they face as many as 150 to 170 students per day?

12. Does a mandatory standardized curriculum turn teachers into lifeless, uninspired repeaters?

13. Do you agree that fewer directives and more support for teachers' inventiveness will keep the best in the profession? Or do you believe that it is dangerous to give teachers this much leeway?

14. Should teachers "teach to the test" or teach to the students' interests and abilities?

15. Why do you think 30 percent of teachers leave the classroom after three years and 50 percent quit after five years?

16. With more than half of the teachers in the classroom today expected to retire in the next six years, how will we have a teacher in every classroom?

17. Would you support higher salaries for teachers, considering their relative standard of living is the lowest it has been in forty years?

18. Do you want computers to replace live teachers for tomorrow's children?

19. How can you encourage good teachers in your school to stay in the profession?

20. In the future, should any college graduate of good character with a passion for teaching be eligible to teach?

## CHAPTER SIX

# So-Called Learning Disabilities

## TEACHING DISABILITIES

Max has come to school with a lingering feeling of discomfort about his dad yelling at him last night. He is hungry again; he always seems to be hungry. He grabbed a donut and coffee on the way to school and now the sugar and caffeine are making him jumpy.

In first period he is fumbling around looking for a pencil, which he knows he doesn't have. He hears the traffic noise outside and smells the stuffiness of the classroom. His eyes catch the girl's hand next to him and he has an impulse to touch her. Her attractiveness pulls on him strongly. At the same time he is aware of the teacher. She is talking and her hands are moving. Max notices that she is feeling the weight of trying to bring the class along with her. Max's toe itches inside his shoe. He wishes he had found clean socks to wear. He is uncomfortable in his body. He can't stand sitting still for another minute so he jumps up to go outside and get a drink of water.

When he returns people are looking at him. He feels awkward and hopes he isn't blushing. The teacher is still talking, but now has a little annoyance in her voice because he has distracted the class. He isn't paying attention as he sits down and he knocks his notebook off the table. The girl next to him smiles. He feels great and then the teacher says, "So, Max, why do you think Prospero caused a shipwreck?" Max doesn't know what she is talking about and wishes he were invisible. He hates school. After lunch he will ditch.

Compare the following scenario with the one above:

Max has come to school with the same issues that he had in the first scenario but as he enters the familiar stuffiness of the classroom, he hears unfamiliar but interesting music. It fills the room with a certain mood, which he can't quite identify. The whole class feels it and he is curious.

The teacher explains that the music is from sixteenth-century England and the class is going to study a play from that era. She asks if the students believe in magic and explains that the play is called *The Tempest* and is about a magician named Prospero and his teenage daughter.

Max reports to his mom when he gets home that day, "We watched a crazy shipwreck scene on video that is the opening of a Shakespeare play. Do you believe in magic? We are going to act out scenes from this play. I play the part of Fernando."

In the first scenario, the teacher reports at the staff meeting that Max never has a pencil with him, is always going outside for a drink, doesn't pay attention, can't contribute to the class, and is failing. The principal reports that Max was absent from afternoon classes and that he (the principal) has put in a call to Max's parents. The staff agrees with Max's teacher that he should be referred to special education. In the second scenario, the teacher reports that Max is participating in class but is struggling with the concentration it takes to read Shakespeare aloud. But he is engaged in acting out the play and learning through the video and music.

Max has been diagnosed as learning-disabled. He has been tested and labeled "LD" (learning disabled). Is this a physiological condition with indications that Max has some sort of organic abnormality? Or is it the result of family, school, or community factors? At this point we don't really know why Max has trouble learning in a focused, linear, and linguistic way. But we do know that Max is smart and aware of most everything going on around him.

We also know that Max is engaged in learning when the lesson includes music, video, and participation on his part. When the *teaching is different,* Max is not "cured" but he is learning. Also the rest of the class is not "held back" by the teaching style that worked for him. The other students are enriched and more engaged as well. It has been our experience that the brightest students are sent soaring in their intellect and creative imagination when they are taught in this enriched style. The students who have stronger academic skills will shine in their written analysis of the material.

There will be no need for Max to be in a special education class, where he may not ever study Shakespeare. Max may execute a fine drawing of the Globe Theatre, portray Fernando with insight and flair, and tune his guitar to sound like a mandolin. Max will contribute to the study of Shakespeare and feel accomplished. Above all, he will learn about the play, the times, and the themes presented in *The Tempest*.

## A Broader Vision of What Learning Requires

How is teaching defined? A common understanding goes something like this:

- Teaching consists of passing information from teacher to student through lecture.
- The student passes the information back to the teacher through testing.
- The test results show what the student has learned.

This model for learning has never been the best. Countless studies have shown that active participation supports learning much better than passive listening, especially for Max. It is impossible for him to learn from lectures at this point in his life. For the rest of the students it is possible to learn from lectures, but is it the best way or the only way to learn?

We propose that real learning requires a broader vision than the lecture/test model, a vision that may empower teachers to provide a meaningful education to every student:

- Learning requires authentic *dialogue,* real human communication based on respect, trust, and partnership.
- Learning requires *student participation.* The student has to feel responsive to the material and have some way of doing, practicing, or responding to it.
- Learning requires a *new understanding*—growth and change that unleash creativity and energy, the energy needed to change the world—as opposed to going over the "same old stuff."
- Learning requires *teaching to the whole student*—physically, emotionally, and mentally—and understanding the student in the context of his or her family, social group, and community.

The vision above sounds great, but you might ask how these requirements of learning relate to a student with learning disabilities such as Max.

In the second scenario of an English class studying Shakespeare's *The Tempest,* the teacher opened the *dialogue* by asking about the Max's views on magic. Max *participated* by assuming a role in scenes from the play. Elizabethan music and culture were *new understandings* that stimulated Max's curiosity and creativity in music, drama, and art. The teacher was *teaching to the whole student* by including art and music with the academic, addressing the physical as well as the mental (acting out scenes), and honoring Max's place in the community by including him and his gifts rather than separating him as "learning-disabled."

## Is a Learning Disability a Disease?

By law, "a learning disability is defined as a significant gap between a person's intelligence and the skills that person has achieved at each age," according to the National Institute of Mental Health report titled *Learning Disabilities*, published in 1993. Does a gap between intelligence and skill sound like a disease to you? According to the definition above, nothing is wrong with the intelligence of someone who has been labeled LD; what is wrong is that he or she has not learned what is expected of him or her.

While specialists are looking inside the kid's brain to locate the source of the problem, we are looking at what is blocking this intelligent child from learning. As we pointed out in the new curriculum, an upset or fearful child is not open to new learning. In our years teaching at Mountain View, every student we encountered who had been diagnosed with a learning disability had personal problems at home. We also witnessed many students who were doing well academically but whose grades dropped dramatically when their parents were getting divorced, when either parent was seriously ill, or when a parent died. Life takes its toll on a child's learning.

Yes, children cope differently with family stress. They also learn differently and at different rates. We can standardize curriculums and tests but we can't standardize students. As was demonstrated in Max's case, children have different strengths and weaknesses. But that does not mean they are disabled. We take issue with this careless labeling of children.

Once this "disability" has been "diagnosed," what is the "cure"? As we somehow expected, all that is needed to cure this "dreaded disease" is different teaching. Unfortunately, most LD-labeled students are now being placed in special education classes, where they theoretically will get the help they need. But many special education programs lack qualified teachers and are overcrowded. In reality, once students are tested and their weaknesses are identified, they are separated from their classmates and placed with other "dummies." As their self-esteem hits bottom, they act out with aggression and hostility or they get depressed. They feel like failures, are labeled "disabled," and often give up hope of amounting to anything. Shame, hostility, and rejection . . . this scenario is a recipe for disaster in many other areas of their lives. We have no argument with the fact that students have specific learning needs. *Every* student has specific learning needs—that is the point.

## SPECIAL EDUCATION CLASSES ARE INAPPROPRIATE

Back in the 1960s the special education class at Richard's school was designed for the small number of students who were truly learning disabled as a result of emotional disturbance, mental retardation, or severe speech and language impediments. During recess he occasionally played with some of these students. There was no question in anyone's mind that they needed a specialized program to help them cope with their learning disabilities. There weren't any students in that class who were simply slow readers or lacked writing skills. This seemed perfectly logical considering the truly special needs of the existing special education students.

This all changed after 1975 with the advent of a federal law that defined a disabled student as one who demonstrates a disorder in the "basic psychological processes involved in understanding or using language." This definition, combined with the inability of scientists to pinpoint any major brain dysfunction among these "disabled" students, resulted in the development of an indirect method for identifying them.

According to an article that appeared in the *Los Angeles Times* titled "Special Education a Failure on Many Fronts," by Richard Lee Colvin and Duke Helfand, educators began administering IQ tests and then measured reading performance to identify students who fit the new category of "learning disabled." If the IQ was significantly higher than the reading score, meaning the child was bright but couldn't read well, they would be designated LD. Thomas Hehir, former director of special education programs for the U.S. Department of Education, was quoted on page 4 of the article as saying, "It's not like diagnosing cancer or heart disease. It's not science. There are lots of kids with reading problems who are not learning disabled."

## Why a Massive Increase in Learning Disabilities?

As a result of this change in the method of classifying learning disabled students, the population in special education classes skyrocketed to 650,000 by 2001 in California alone, according to Alice Parker, California director of special education, encompassing about one in ten public school students. Classes that were originally designed to teach the 2 percent to 5 percent of students who had true physical and mental disabilities and who would be lost intellectually in a regular class have now been swollen by the ranks of children who merely demonstrate trouble in reading and writing skills. These ranks have grown by 63 percent in California over the past fifteen years. Alice Parker, California's director of special education, stated in the above-mentioned *Los Angeles Times* article that as many as 250,000 students with reading difficulties shouldn't be in special education classes.

G. Reid Lyon, head of the federal government's research efforts into reading and learning disabilities, also claimed on page 1 of the article that "'learning disabled' has become the sociological sponge to wipe up the spills of general education." Many educators, researchers, and even a California state task force are now saying that the biggest factor driving the growth in the number of learning disabled students is poor general education instruction, especially in reading. The state task force found that a significant number of children labeled "learning disabled" or "dyslexic" could have become successful readers had they received systemic and explicit instruction and intervention far earlier in their educational careers. Educators now realize that the phasing out of phonics in California in the late 1980s also resulted in a dramatic increase in special education students.

## The Massive Increase in Special Education Classes

In effect, special education has become a dumping ground for students with reading difficulties and behavior problems. Stressed-out teachers in crowded classes may think they are actually doing struggling students a favor by transferring them to less crowded special education classes. But with a severe shortage of resources and lack of qualified teachers willing to take on the complex problems of special education, students are often left to languish and fall further behind.

For these students, special education can become, according to page 2 of the *Los Angeles Times* article cited above, "a trap of inappropriately slowed down instruction, lowered goals and a lifetime of stigma."

According to the U.S. Department of Education, Office of Special Education Programs, Data Analysis System, there was a 36.6 percent increase in learning disabled students attending U.S. public schools between 1990 and 1999 (2001). Students in special education classes are three times more likely to have untrained teachers and twice as likely to drop out prior to graduation than their mainstream peers. Unfortunately, the numbers of special education students are predicted to rise as many of the recent educational reforms are implemented. These include the tough accountability measures that can force closure of schools that do not achieve high scores on standardized tests. One way to avoid low test scores is to place "underachievers" in special education classes, where their test scores aren't counted.

## Teaching to a Low IQ

So far we have focused on the 50 percent of special education students who are considered learning disabled because of a gap between their IQ test performance and their demonstrated skills in reading and writing. What about the other 50 percent? These are students who are enrolled in special education because of mental disability, autism, and speech and language impediments such as stuttering.

These children are experiencing true learning disabilities that require special teachers and expertise. Teachers who work with the truly learning disabled are trained to use methods to help these children learn basic skills. The methods include drill, repetition and practice, sequencing (breaking down the task into parts), and systematic questioning.

What happens when the so-called learning disabled students who simply need help with their reading are placed in special education classes where these techniques are being used? The unfortunate consequence is that their boredom and anxiety levels increase when they have to endure an entire school day focused on drill and repetition designed for the mentally or emotionally disadvantaged. They fall further behind and don't get the creative stimulation they need to move forward with their learning. Many of the students in special education classes are not mentally disadvantaged. In fact, many hyperactive kids directed into special education have very high IQs. How are they doing in a class that is full of drill and repetition?

## RESULTS OF LEARNING DISABILITY DIAGNOSIS

It can be a terrible defeat for a child to be stuck with a label like learning disabled. The high school years are so much about peer approval and acceptance that the label LD can become a stigma that often turns into a permanent disadvantage. Parents who are desperate to find a cure for their child's inability to succeed in school should be very cautious about accepting the diagnosis of learning disabled. Quite often, difficulties in learning can be overcome through tutoring, placing the child in a school offering smaller classes and more individual attention or more support at home. We should never underestimate the damage to self-esteem the label LD can do to a child and how much it compounds other issues associated with a difficulty in reading or writing.

### The LD Label Can Be a Tremendous Defeat

We recently heard about a young woman who grew up with the dream of becoming a kindergarten teacher. But she was slow learning to read in elementary school and was shuffled into special education, where she stayed permanently behind her former classmates. She never received the kind of help that would have enabled her to catch up with her reading and rejoin her classmates. After graduation the young woman went to work in a fast food restaurant and her dream of becoming a teacher seemed hopelessly beyond her grasp.

The repercussions of being placed in special education are often permanent. Consider these statistics:

- According to a California state task force study that examined special education, fewer than 10 percent of children who are saddled with the learning disabled label ever leave special education.
- According to the National Longitudinal Transition study funded by the U.S. Department of Education's office of Special Education Programs, 38 percent of children with learning disabilities drop out of high school, twice the normal rate. Fewer than 2 percent attend a four-year college.
- According to the Educational Resources Information Center (ERIC) Clearing House on Disabilities, youths with disabilities experience a substantially higher substance abuse risk than their nondisabled peers.

## A Learning Disability Is a Good Excuse

Many teens will work every angle to their benefit if they can. Some of the students who had been diagnosed with leaning disabilities before coming to our high school used their diagnosis as an excuse for every shortfall, from not remembering to do their homework to being late to class. It gave them a handy reason for any lack of discipline or responsibility for their own success or failure.

We dropped every label as soon as a student entered our school. We held every student to the same standards. We recognized that the quality of a student's work would vary with the personal level of skill combined with the individual's inherent ability. But we required that every student work to his or her level and we maintained high expectations. Some tried to use the old LD label to get out of doing homework or to do minimal work. They had become accustomed to a lack of academic effort and accountability. Consistent higher expectations had the effect of putting them back on track.

The label of "hyper" leads to a denial of self-mastery. If students are given this label, they will tell you that they have to get up several times during class, that they have to talk during assembly, and that they will forget that skateboard riding is not allowed on campus. The label makes the shortcomings in behavior justifiable to them.

We did work with these kids as they arrived at our school. One very athletic girl told Ellen after class that she was so restless during class that she could hardly sit still. Ellen could see that she was sincere and working to succeed at her new school. We discussed it and agreed that an occasional lap around the building would help her. We agreed on a signal that she would use to tell Ellen that she needed a lap. It was an escape valve that she rarely used, but just knowing it was there eased her tension. After she settled into the school, the run became unnecessary. We are not suggesting that every classroom needs a running track around it, only that individual students can be worked with in the classroom in an individual way to overcome their personal challenges.

## The Learning Disability Industry

A huge and thriving industry has developed around learning disabilities. Parents are told to get professional help, which may include some or all of the following:

- Counseling for the student
- Counseling for the family
- Joining a support group
- Purchasing self-help books written by educators or mental health professionals
- Hiring a tutor
- Seeing a physician to obtain a prescription drug for hyperactivity

These expensive "treatments" will not result in the "patient" being "cured," but he or she may improve.

In order to gauge the size of this industry, it is necessary to identify the number of children with symptoms to be diagnosed and treated. We present here a few statistics:

- According to the U.S. Department of Education, 2.8 million students are currently receiving special education services for learning disabilities in the United States (2000).
- According to the National Institute of Child Health and Development, 20 percent of students cannot master reading without special help, and approximately 85 percent of all individuals with learning disabilities have difficulty in the area of reading (2001).

The numbers of kids with learning disabilities increases when we include those served in private schools, treated in private medical or other therapeutic practice, and privately tutored. What kinds of services and products are being produced for these millions?

- Universities are offering degrees in special education and are therefore buying texts, training professors, developing curriculum, and the like.
- Universities and government health and education departments are producing research on the "learning disabled."
- Testing companies are producing and selling assessment systems and screening tests.
- Therapists and counselors are being trained in treating those who "suffer" from learning disability "symptoms."
- Writers are producing manuals for teachers and student curriculum materials for special education classes.
- Publishers are producing curriculum materials and teacher training materials for special education classes.

- Drug companies are producing Ritalin and other drugs and advertising and selling them.
- Physicians and pediatricians in particular are seeing "patients" with "symptoms" to be "diagnosed" and treated with drugs.
- Various colleges are promoting themselves as especially suited for the learning disabled.
- A World Congress and Exposition has been established for learning disabilities.
- Attorneys are now specializing in learning disability issues.
- Videos are available to give parents advice on advocacy and support issues.

This is an amazing phenomenon when we consider that the rise in learning disabilities is correlated with the phasing out of phonics in the early 1980s and the advent of a diagnosis that broadened the definition of LD to include a lack of skills in reading and writing. The response has far outweighed the actual problem. If we focused our attention on smaller class size and promoting creative and innovative methods of teaching that appeal to a child's curiosity and natural ability to learn, we could deal more effectively with so-called learning disabilities and spend less money.

## ADD/ADHD

Winston was a precocious young boy who struggled with reading and writing in school. His parents didn't have the time or patience to help him so they arranged for him to attend a boarding school, where they hoped he would settle down and apply himself. Matters only got worse as Winston became homesick and agitated and began acting up in order to get the attention he craved. But his parents had found what they considered a suitable place for him, so they all but abandoned him to the school.

Winston was smaller than his classmates and slightly overweight. He was picked on and earned the reputation of an academic and behavioral misfit. Finally when he turned thirteen Winston was assigned a tutor, who worked with him to help him improve his reading skills. The tutor also introduced him to the classics of literature and Winston became an avid reader.

But as Winston grew to young adulthood and reached the point in his education where he had to decide whether to pursue a higher education or join the work force, he opted to join the military, not having earned the grades needed to be accepted into a university. But Winston Churchill went on to become the highest-paid foreign correspondent in the world and eventually chose politics as a career, leading the British in their victory against Nazi Germany.

If Sir Winston were a schoolboy today, he would undoubtedly be diagnosed with attention deficit hyperactivity disorder (ADHD), and probably dyslexia as well. He exhibited all the ADHD symptoms: fidgeting, losing things, aggressive behavior, and difficulty reading. But many of young Winston's problems stemmed from his family circumstances, with parents who rarely spent time together and even less time with him. The saving grace for Winston Churchill was the tutor who introduced him to literature and worked with him one-on-one until he mastered the craft of writing. He went on to author one of the most respected histories of the English-speaking people and was a gifted and witty orator.

When we add the names Henry Ford, Albert Einstein, Alexander Graham Bell, Leonardo da Vinci, and Michelangelo, we not only have a list of famous men who exhibited symptoms of dyslexia and ADHD, but we also have a list of some of the most brilliant and inventive minds the world has ever known. These men didn't allow their supposed "handicap" to keep them from accomplishing great things. They may have been considered poor students, they may have been ridiculed, but they all connected with something they excelled in. At some point in their lives they all were encouraged by someone who believed in them and were urged to pursue their dreams.

## The Diagnosis of ADD/ADHD

Don't "hyper" children with attention deficit disorder (ADD) or ADHD have something wrong with their brain chemistry? The answer is that the diagnosis of these two disorders is accomplished by observing behavior only. There is no chemical test, no blood test, no neurological test for ADD or ADHD. Yes, it's true.

According to the National Institute of Mental Health's booklet *Learning Disabilities* (1993), page 8, available on the Internet at www.nimh.nih.gov, "ADHD is diagnosed by checking for the long-term presence of specific behaviors, such as considerable fidgeting, losing things, interrupting, and talking excessively. Other signs include an inability to remain seated, stay on task, or take turns." The fact is that the diagnosis for the "disorder" of ADD/ADHD is purely behavioral. The professional observes and makes note of specific behaviors and then determines that the disorders exist and often prescribes a drug treatment. There is no evidence of an organic disease, no brain chemistry imbalance, no virus, no bacteria, no physical defect, nothing but behavior.

## Drugged for Behavior Problems

What makes the ADD/ADHD diagnosis so serious is that the treatment is often prescription drugs: 75 percent of those children diagnosed with ADD/ADHD are given Ritalin or a similar drug.

According to Congressional testimony given by Terrance Woodworth, deputy director of the U.S. Drug Enforcement Administration, the number of prescriptions written to treat ADD/ADHD has increased 500 percent since 1991, as reported by *Education World* news editor Diane Weaver. For nearly six decades, children have been prescribed drugs for "attention disorders," hyperactive behaviors, and impulsiveness. The drugs are Ritalin (methylphenidate), Dexedrine (dextroamphetamine), and Cylert (pemoline). They are stimulants in the category of "speed" and "diet pills" that temporarily improve children's attention and ability to focus, and 90 percent of kids given these drugs calm down and pay better attention in school.

We agree that the drugs work. Students calm down and are better able to pay attention, but at what cost? These drugs are not a solution to the problem but a relief of the symptoms. In a few hours, after the drug wears off, the symptoms are back. Stimulants are addictive drugs and children are learning that a drug can solve their problems. This is not a constructive message to give them.

## A Deficit in Attention

There is no reason why children who have been diagnosed with these so-called learning disabilities can't live out their dreams. They simply need someone to pay attention to them and their ideas. Attention deficit disorder is just that—no one is paying the proper attention to them.

It is no wonder in today's fast-paced world, where both parents often work, that there is an epidemic of ADD and ADHD. With so much of our learning taking place in the home, it's easy to understand how children develop these deficiencies. If we really want to address the causes of attention deficit, we need to examine the quality of the whole environment the child experiences on a daily basis.

Is the child growing up in an environment of emotional stability in the home, or is the home a battleground between warring parents? Often the home is also a place where a silent form of hostility results in neglect of the child. By examining aboriginal cultures, we find that the way children learn is through imitating their parents. They learn through observation and imitation—by acting things out, asking questions, and sharing information with their peers.

Children raised in emotionally and intellectually nurturing environments in which at least one parent is present to respond to their hunger for learning have a far greater chance of avoiding the label of ADD/ADHD once they reach school age. Studies have also identified a direct correlation between the incidence of learning disabilities and the amount of time children spend in childcare facilities away from their parents. Emotional stability, open communication, and a home environment conducive to learning will pave the way to a successful school experience. Children raised in such an environment will be free of the struggle to get the attention they so deeply crave.

### Stressed Out

How productive are we when we are upset or stressed? Do we shuffle things around, lose things, have trouble paying attention, become aggressive? Or do we withdraw and turn to some kind of feel-good remedy like alcohol or tranquilizers? Children who exhibit symptoms associated with attention deficit disorder are demonstrating these same symptoms, symptoms of being stressed out. No wonder they have difficulty learning.

In our years at Mountain View High School we had many opportunities to observe students who'd been diagnosed with ADD and ADHD. Invariably and without exception, we were able to connect these so-called learning disabilities to things that were amiss in the child's environment.

For many years now a cadre of educational experts and researchers have been saying that learning involves a wide range of inputs and experiences, and that learning, growing, and daily life are so closely related that to separate them is to miss what constitutes real education. A child's learning experience is an integrated whole that includes his or her home life and experiences in the community. If we make that environment as healthy and nurturing as possible, we will be in a much better position to help our children overcome many perceived learning disabilities:

Roger enrolled in our school as a ninth grader. He was a very quiet and withdrawn boy who had difficulty answering the simple questions we posed to him during his initial interview. His reading and writing skills were a year or two below the ninth-grade level.

In class Roger was operating in a fog, unable to comprehend the lessons and unable to participate in class discussions. Roger's parents told us that they were also having trouble with their oldest daughter. She was getting into trouble in school and hanging out with the wrong crowd and they were afraid Roger was going to follow the same pattern. When he'd been diagnosed with ADD, it was recommended that he take Ritalin.

But there seemed to be more to Roger's story than merely his problems with reading, writing, and paying attention. During his initial interview we perceived a strain of tension between his parents. Their inability to agree on how to handle the problems with Roger and his older sister was clearly contributing to a stressful family dynamic.

Although we really liked Roger and tried our best to help him feel welcome at the school, he wasn't able to break out of the fog that seemed to be clouding his perceptive and communicative abilities. That year might have been the end of our association with Roger, because the following year his parents decided to enroll him in a remedial education program. But the next summer Roger's parents contacted us again, asking if we would consider readmitting him for his eleventh-grade year. After assuring us over the phone that Roger was in much better shape, he showed up at his enrollment interview a changed person.

No longer quiet and withdrawn, Roger was now playing tennis and working part time. Both parents accompanied Roger to this interview and the tension we felt at the first interview seemed to have vanished. We allowed Roger to reenroll with the stipulation that he continue working and playing tennis.

As a junior, Roger bloomed in the community atmosphere of our school. We were amazed at the changes that had taken place in him. Although he still exhibited reading difficulties and some trouble with his writing, he was alive, engaged, and eager to succeed in his classes. He began writing poetry, demonstrated mastery of the computer, and kept everyone laughing with his jokes and puns. Something had stabilized for Roger that enabled him to succeed at our school.

Later we reflected on this and realized Roger's personal growth had much to do with his parents having resolved their relationship difficulties so they could provide a more supportive home environment. We also credited them with caring enough about him to help him back into a school that would help draw out his positive qualities.

Roger had discovered a way to feel good about himself and it resulted in his successful completion of high school. He formed many friendships with the teachers and students at our school and was reluctant to leave when graduation day finally arrived.

## WHAT TO DO

What are you to do when the school or the counselor informs you that your child has been diagnosed as learning disabled or ADD/ADHD? We recommend that you ask to see the test results. If the diagnosis is based on a discrepancy between the IQ and achievement of the child and not due to neurological problems, physical problems, or a low IQ, then your job is clearly defined. You need to help bring your child's achievement level up to what is appropriate for his or her grade level.

If the diagnosis is based on the behaviors associated with hyperactivity, we suggest that you take a close look at how you can improve your child's home life. How can you reduce the stress in your child's life? A counselor may help you and your family, or a change in schools may help, depending on the source of the stress.

### Resist the Label for Your Child

Children with a diagnosis of learning disabled are often not working to their potential. As we have argued previously, we do not see these students as disabled in any way but as bright kids who aren't learning in school. If the label of learning disabled is resisted, the solutions look quite manageable. We shall look carefully at them in this section.

Although our discussion is about teenagers in this book, the diagnosis of ADD and ADHD comes earlier in most students' lives and dramatically affects their high school career. Because this label of "hyperactivity" or ADD/ADHD can be so damaging, we recommend that parents resist the label as well. The following typical story of a real boy says it better than we ever could:

Andrew had a difficult birth and required physical therapy as a toddler and preschooler to relax the taut muscles in one of his limbs. His mother, who was single, was overwhelmed by the physical difficulties this unexpected baby presented. But she was devoted to Andrew's well-being. Andrew's biological father stayed in the background and offered little support financially or emotionally.

Andrew was a beautiful boy, talkative and imaginative. He had unquenchable curiosity and enthusiasm. When Ellen first met him he was one of those kids who could tell you the names and vital statistics of every known dino-saur. Andrew's mother shared with Ellen the problems he had in school. Andrew did not like doing things over and over again. Once he had a math problem figured out, he couldn't understand why he had to waste his time doing twenty of the same problem. Being highly verbal, he was eager to give the right answer, persistent with questions, and proud to let you know what he knew about everything. He needed a lot of attention and was a "high-maintenance" kid for any teacher.

Tedious skills that required repetition or worksheets were troublesome. He hated homework because it cut into playtime, and his reading level was a little behind the class. In private preschool, his teacher had recommended Ritalin and the director of the school had agreed that it would calm him down, slow him down, and quiet him down. His mother resisted this sug-gestion instinctively, although she knew that Andrew was a handful for the teacher. But he was a smart, good-natured, and happy boy. Mom did not agree that the drug was the solution.

Moving to public school and larger classrooms only exacerbated Andrew's excitability and eagerness to talk. But he was gaining more self-control with his mother's encouragement and his teacher's persistence. And then the ter-rible day came when the school called Andrew's mother to give her the di-agnosis of learning disabilities. Andrew was devastated, because he thought he was smart. Mom read everything she could find about LD and visited the pediatrician as the school recommended. The prescription for Ritalin was written for Andrew.

But Andrew's mother again resisted the diagnosis. She asked Andrew's teacher what it would take for Andrew to stay in the regular classroom and not be sent to special education. The teacher said that his reading level must go up and he must become less disruptive by not talking as much and by working quietly at his desk more. She gave Andrew a three-month reprieve, in which time Mom hired a reading tutor and set up a system of conse-quences for Andrew's class behavior. Every afternoon when she picked him up from school, she asked the teacher how he had done that day. His read-ing level came up and his behavior improved, but to this day Andrew still requires constant monitoring and coaching from Mom.

We suspect that if Andrew's mother had not resisted the learning disabled label, Andrew would have been "calmer," "better behaved," and "easier to handle" on Ritalin for a few years. But by the time he would have arrived at high school, Andrew would have been sullen, feeling "dumb," hating school, and causing trouble. Andrew would no longer demand our constant atten-tion. His personality would have been successfully altered, his enthusiastic response to life dampened.

Because our alternative high school had small classes with personal attention and individualized instruction, many parents came to us with "learning disabled" children. We were what the doctor ordered to "save" their kids. We were not a school for the learning disabled, but about 30 percent of the student body had some diagnosis of learning difficulty. A combination of high IQ and learning disabled kids make up the student body of many alternative high schools.

We saw many kids like Andrew who were not as fortunate and had gone down the Ritalin road or special education road. Over the many years, we helped them as they struggled to regain their self-esteem and rediscover their inherent intelligence and gifts. We were able to turn some lives around and share the joy of a young life found again. Some we were not able to help.

### Find a Supportive Learning Environment

Many school districts provide an alternative school for problem teenagers in their districts. These schools range from glorified teenage baby-sitting to premier innovative, dynamic learning centers. Parents need to know that just because a district offers an alternative, it may not be the place for their child. Private schools, if affordable, are not necessarily any better. They range from attentive, compassionate, supportive environments to cutthroat, competitive pressure cookers.

So what should a parent look for? We suggest a parent visit various schools and see if the students are happy. This may sound simplistic, but it is the best measurement. A hyperactive teenager will need to be in a relaxed and supportive environment if he or she is going to raise his or her skill level or channel his or her hyperactivity into creative learning. Teens with hyperactivity or attention deficit issues also need a secure environment where limits are clearly defined. No student is happy in a free-for-all.

The best option is a school that focuses on strengths rather than weaknesses. One mother we knew enrolled her son in a private high school that had a great music program, as her son was a gifted guitar player. Another parent found a school that offered an elective in marine biology; his daughter was able to conduct field studies in the ocean, which she loved. As we will describe in Chapter 8, parents have many options.

### Hire a Tutor for LD

If you receive word that your child is not keeping up academically, get a tutor right away. Many skills are incremental and build on one another. If a step in reading or mathematics is missed because your child had the flu, he or she might be lost in the subject from that point on. Or perhaps your child has an academic weakness in one specific subject. Don't let your child slide below grade level without trying to help. Don't assume that the school will take care of it. Schools are overburdened with too many kids in a class, too much to teach, and too little help. Hire a good tutor.

Our daughter had a first-grade teacher who used a newly adopted reading program that required the students to guess how a word was spelled and then write their guess on the board. Our daughter was miserable. She wanted to know how it was really spelled, not guess at it. And she was too shy to go to the board. By the time we figured out what was going on, she was considered "slow." She had also missed much of what she needed to learn about reading in the first grade because she was so emotionally upset.

We placed her in a school with a much better teacher-student ratio and hired a tutor to help her catch up. The new school also informed us that she was "slow to learn and behind the rest of her class." In a few months the tutor had identified the missing skills and taught them to her. She flew forward in her learning and is now near the top of her class and doing exceptionally well in twelfth-grade advanced placement English. If we had accepted the diagnosis that our daughter was a slow learner, this exceptionally bright girl could have ended up languishing in special education and would have never reached her potential.

## Protect Your Family from ADD

Hyperactivity has been blamed on our rapid-fire culture, food additives, sibling rivalry, poor teachers, and caffeine, to name just a few things. These things may contribute to hyperactivity, but when a student with a normal IQ can't sit still, can't pay attention, can't focus enough to remember to bring a pencil and paper, he or she is essentially distracted. Something is so disturbing or upsetting that the student can't concentrate on what is in front of him or her.

The home and family are the base from which a child launches him- or herself into the world. Step by step he or she is advancing from childhood toward adulthood. Home is where an adolescent returns after forays into the broader community as an independent person. Home can be a quiet place for reflection, a supportive talk with an adult, or nourishing food and a good sleep.

What if home is a place of fear, chaos, anger, and loneliness? The teenager will be unhappy because he or she is not feeling secure about parental support or about his or her own worthiness to be independent. Can a teenager face the challenges of his or her coming of age with a dysfunctional home life? At the very least the teenager will have to go to school. If he or she is deeply unsettled about home life, an inability to focus on schoolwork will probably persist.

As in Andrew's case, often parents are doing all they can to help their children and improve their own lives. Single parents especially have a lot to juggle. But anything that can be done to provide a stable, supportive home life will make a tremendous difference to a child who is dealing with hyperactivity.

## TWENTY QUESTIONS FOR PARENTS

1. Do you know for certain or suspect that your child has learning disabilities? If yes, these questions are for you.
2. Do you feel it is your problem or the school's problem?
3. As learning disabilities are diagnosed solely through the observation of behavior, do you consider LD a disease or a behavior problem?
4. Is your child in a special education class due to learning disabilities?
5. Does your child have difficulty reading, leaving him or her at risk of being labeled learning disabled?
6. Do you know if your child was taught phonics (sounding out words) when learning to read?
7. Are you experiencing desperation in finding a solution to your child's inability to succeed in school?
8. Have you tried the option of tutoring in phonics for reading difficulties?
9. Does your child feel defeated by the label learning disabled?
10. Have you searched for an educational setting where the label for your child would be dropped?
11. Has your child's learning disability incurred expenses for you such as testing, consultation, tutoring, or counseling?
12. If your child has been diagnosed with ADD/ADHD, does he or she know of the geniuses and creative inventors that shared the same symptoms?
13. Are you happy with the standard prescription of Ritalin or the like for students with hyperactivity?

14. If your child has been diagnosed with ADD, has he or she been getting enough of the right attention?

15. Is there anything you can do as a parent to strengthen the environment your child lives in, physically, emotionally, or mentally?

16. Do you have a clear direction for what to do about your child's diagnosis of LD or ADD/ADHD?

17. Is your child in a supportive learning environment for his or her learning style?

18. Does your child's learning environment or school focus on his or her strengths rather than weaknesses?

19. If your child has been diagnosed with a learning disability from the school, have you considered hiring a tutor?

20. If your child has been diagnosed with ADD/ADHD, have you considered family counseling to help identify the instability in his or her life?

## CHAPTER SEVEN

# The School as Community

Carla became pregnant in the summer between her junior and senior year. She had a regretful sexual encounter at a party with a boy she hardly knew and refused to tell anyone who he was. With her mother's support Carla decided to have her baby and that they would raise the baby together. But how would she deal with her last year of high school?

When Carla's "situation" became known at school, the students came together and decided that as a community they would help her any way they could. As her due date got closer, the students shared her excitement of baby kicks and comforted her with back massages. The girls gave her a baby shower. "How's our baby doing in there?" the kids would ask. Carla was encouraged to keep up her grades and not let the pregnancy deter her from her academic goals. She'd known since she was a little girl that she wanted to be a doctor. She possessed the intellectual capability and discipline to achieve her dream but could have suffered a tragic defeat without the support she received from the school community.

When the baby was a month old, she brought him to school for part of a day. And Carla brought her beautiful son to graduation.

This may seem like an unusual response coming from a group of teenagers. Even the teachers at our school were surprised at how Carla was totally accepted and nurtured instead of being made fun of and rejected. But when a school is small enough, teens can share each other's dreams in a culture of caring and acceptance.

## WHY IS COMMUNITY IMPORTANT?

An educational community can provide support for its members to succeed. But it has to be small and intimate enough for everyone to *know* each other's needs. The call has been going out for well over a decade to create smaller schools capable of providing caring communities for our teenagers

In its seminal report *Turning Points*, the Carnegie Council on Adolescent Development (1989) called for schools to "provide small-scale communities for learning." The section titled "Meeting Essential Requirements for Healthy Adolescent Development" (available at www.carnegie.org) recognized that "close, trusting relationships among faculty and students give rise to a climate that stimulates growth and intellectual development." The report advocated the shrinking of schools so that students can rely on a small, caring group of teachers to offer well-coordinated and meaningful educational experiences. It also supported small school communities that allow teachers to really get to know and understand their students, so they can respond to them as individuals.

It is absolutely vital for the well-being of our culture to create the sense of a caring community in the high school. During these four years teenagers are learning how to function in a social group. We abhor cliques, but what do we offer as an alternative? What are we teaching our teens about living successfully in community? When we put teens behind chain-link fences in huge schools isolated from the surrounding neighborhood, tell them not to talk in class, and limit their ability to communicate with their teachers and administrators, how can we expect them to learn what a caring community is all about?

## Need to Belong

The beliefs and attitudes of peers become extremely important at this stage of life. The peer group whom teenagers choose will be influential in deciding their ideas, values, and lifestyles. How many times have we heard parents say, "She started hanging around with the wrong group of kids; that's why she got into trouble"? Peer groups have a tremendous influence during this time, as teens tend to distance themselves from the family circle.

An issue of equal concern to teenagers is wanting to know if they are attractive to the opposite sex. Teens want to know what it means to be male or female in the culture and how to successfully project attractiveness. A school community can be a much better place to explore the nuances of sexual identity than looking for answers in teen magazines, on television, or in the movies. In a school community teens can explore their identity based on friendships and casual inter-actions with the opposite sex. They can enjoy each other's company even if they don't all look like superstars.

The cliques that evolve at most large high schools are often based on attractiveness. Being rejected or not included in a clique can wreak havoc on teenage sexual identity. Cliques do not form as readily when a school is small enough for the faculty to actively promote inclusive-ness. In a small, inclusive school community there isn't as much pres-sure to "couple up." In schools where a sense of community is encouraged, teens tend to hang out together in a large, loosely knit group.

A small school community can also provide the social, emotional, and intellectual support (and challenges) that every student needs. The people who make up the community—fellow students, teachers, and administrators—can help define beliefs, support beliefs, challenge be-liefs, or question beliefs for a teenager. The community can help a student through an emotional challenge such as an illness, accident, divorce, or death in the family. But finally and most importantly for most students, the community provides a social setting for teens to gain skills at making friends and socializing with their peers.

A community is by its nature inclusive. It follows that a commu-nity does not exclude "nerds" or any other group. Yet in most high schools there are a variety of exclusive groups or cliques.

## Cliques

Being all alone in a school of thousands of students can be over-whelming and very lonely. Students group together in an effort to belong, to explore their identity, and to feel safe enough to develop socially. Teens are trying to form an identity away from family. It is good to feel like you belong to something. Cliques that form in high school include some variations of the following:

*"Preppies"* sport the collegiate look with brand name labels. They are headed for college, preferably the Ivy League.

*"Jocks"* are athletes and often the most popular.

*"Ravers"* are the partiers. They like body piercing, short skirts or baggy clothes, glitter makeup, and "bedhead" hairdos.

*"Nerds"* are way smart, but not very "cool."

*"Hackers or Techies"* are into computers and little else. They speak their own
   cyberlanguage.
*"Goths"* wear all black, try to be totally grim, and act like social misfits.
*"Skaters"* wear skateboard T-shirts, baggy shorts, baseball caps, and skater
   shoes and are whizzing off to the skate park every chance they get.

Although these colorful teenage cliques are enjoyable to read about,
the tragedy is that cliques often reject and even shun those who are
not members or members who fall out of favor. The desperation of
those who are rejected should not be taken lightly. The shooters at
Columbine were teased unmercifully by different cliques and were
quoted as saying, "This is for all the people who made fun of us all
these years" as they opened fire in the cafeteria.

   Other teens have said that being teased for how they dressed made
them not want to go to school. A girl who does not keep up with the
fashion because she can't afford it may be dropped from a clique. A
preppy whose grades start to fall may be shunned by other preppies:
"We don't want a loser like you hanging around with us." When the
motto is "conform or be ridiculed," a society produces tyrants, ter-
rorists, and loners and therefore a selfish and lonely world.

   Members of one clique may "hate" those in other cliques without
even knowing them. This kind of stereotyping, rivalry, and unques-
tioned and unneeded hatred is a destructive habit. Do we want our
children thinking in such a limited way? How do we expect them to
create a peaceful world to live in?

   We believe that the solution to this culture of cliques is smaller
schools with lots of interaction between the students so they get to
know each other. In a small school a student can be a unique individual and may not need to cling to a clique such as the ones listed
above. If students can be part of a small community, they don't have
to wear one of these confining identities. Some students enjoy experi-
menting with different personalities. A student can wear many hats:
he or she may be into studying for college, the latest computer technology, skateboarding, playing basketball, and going to parties.

   Again we repeat the theme that small schools with a strong inclusive community are better for teens. Here's a story about a student
who felt supported enough by the school community to try out a series
of identities.

Andy's grades were outstanding during his first year of high school and he was
popular with the other students. He was a pure joy to have in a classroom,

contributing insight and humor into every discussion. But as the months wore on, Andy began to try on different personas. His conservative clothing acquired a ragged edge and eventually he was coming to school with safety pins holding his jeans together. Gradually he moved into khaki pants and a cable-knit sweater and one day he came to school in a white suit. This look was followed by an array of working-class T-shirts, including those advertising a trucking company and a dry-cleaning service. When he graced our performance night wearing tattered cowboy boots, a sweat-stained hat, and plaid shirt and sang an original country western song, no one was surprised.

The transformations were always complete. His language was slightly modified and his posture changed as he became the persona he was trying on. His classmates never made much of his changes other than a few raised eyebrows at the white suit. He was free to be an outrageous adolescent and try on as many personas as he wanted.

## Today's Students Will Create the World

The strife in our world today has much to do with the process of exclusion. One of the many examples is Northern Ireland, where Catholic kids need the protection of armed guards as they walk to school through Protestant neighborhoods.

If our goal as educators is to help promote peace and harmony, then we can begin by promoting inclusiveness and acceptance in our schools. The aspect of inclusiveness could actually be viewed as an imperative, an evolutionary leap for humankind that will ensure our ultimate survival. The first step in this evolutionary process is to encourage a sense of inclusiveness among students.

To have a social conscience, to live beyond personal fulfillment, to understand that every part affects the whole is what inclusiveness is all about. Inclusiveness doesn't mean conformity, but it does mean tolerance for differences and taking responsibility for the welfare of all members of the group. Where will our young people learn these principles if not in school where they are in a group? Can teens be taught to recognize their fellow students and teachers as individuals with unique personalities, problems, and gifts?

## HOW TO CREATE COMMUNITY IN A HIGH SCHOOL

The whole school can become a community when it is small enough and when the intention to do so is clear. At Mountain View High School we were small and we intentionally created community.

The intention to have a community is critical. Community building is not happenstance. We constantly had to work at it. We told our students that we had to come together to support each other. We made "kindness" a requirement and stressed it in the student handbook. Although it was clear that the students didn't all like each other, they were expected to be kind and respectful, both to students and to teachers.

In class discussions we encouraged different opinions but demanded that every opinion be respected. "Dissing" or "trashing" each other was not accepted as a legitimate response in a discussion. We encouraged students to help rather than compete with each other. We avoided promoting the high academic achievers as the students we were most proud of. Instead we recognized each student for his or her unique gifts and efforts. Every student received an award at the end of the year, not just the brilliant ones.

For many incoming students these new skills of respect for every individual had to be learned. Divisions and feuds flared up regularly as new students slowly and sometimes painfully learned how to cope with the climate of caring and inclusiveness that we promoted. We needed to continually monitor this climate so that everyone understood that it was inappropriate to tease and harass. But the prevailing school culture was always moving toward a supportive community. Trying to hold this ideal for the campus reminded Ellen of the definition of straight and level flight as being "a constant series of minor corrections."

In a school community students need continual social contact with each other so that they can learn more about each other. School administrators should promote a variety of activities for the entire student body that bring the school community together. At Mountain View we used the school bulletin board to announce student successes and opportunities, display jokes, and share job possibilities, news articles, and upcoming school events. An easel was also placed at the entrance to school with a quote written on it each day. These quotes from rock stars, writers, philosophers, and comics were the basis for a contest. The first student to guess the source of the quote received a fountain pen at the weekly assembly. Sometimes the students themselves would offer a quote for the day. This practice served many purposes. It brought a little challenge and excitement to the start of each day and it also got the whole school thinking about a particular inspirational idea or funny phrase.

Here's a story about how we intentionally created a greater sense of community in our school:

During Richard's first year as a high school teacher he rarely saw his colleagues except at staff meetings. They came and went from their respective classes like ships passing in the night. They were all on friendly terms and enjoyed each other, but there wasn't a way to spend much time together or share information on a daily basis. It was the same with the students. Richard had great relationships with the kids in his classes but didn't have a chance to interact with the other students in the school.

The following year, when he joined the administration, Richard wanted to do something about this lack of cohesiveness in the school community. He could see the possibilities of having a weekly assembly that enhanced the feeling of community, but big changes would have to be made in the usual routine to get them there.

He'd read in an article about ice cream entrepreneurs Ben Cohen and Jerry Greenfield, who had started what they called a "Joy Committee" for their company employees in order to create a more supportive company culture. They celebrated birthdays, encouraged their employees to make announcements at the staff meetings, and promoted a more inclusive and equitable environment between management and staff.

Richard felt the school needed to bring something like the Joy Committee to the assemblies, so he completely transformed the assembly. First he awarded a pen to any student who had guessed the daily quote and then encouraged them to make any kind of announcement they wanted before the teachers made theirs. They could report on some school project they were working on, like a car wash or a dance, or share some music or poetry. He launched the Joy Committee music tradition by bringing his saxophone to school and playing a jazz number, generating enthusiastic cheers and applause.

Gradually the Joy Committee caught on and every week a student would read a poem, play a song, or bring along a tape of his or her favorite music to share. The school eventually expanded the Joy Committee to include birthday celebrations. The administrators always held the official school announcements till the end of the assembly.

This restructuring transformed the assembly from a dreary affair to a genuine community forum. The teachers who attended were able to share information with the students and each other. The students became much more involved in school activities and the weekly gathering served a more vibrant and vital function.

After the first year of instituting the Joy Committee Richard felt much more connected with the students and teachers. The simple act of sharing information in a fun and creative way established links for them all.

A high school is essentially a community of learning and teaching. Loners miss the boat in a high school. We see the high school community as a series of connecting circles, similar to the Olympics logo, that connects students with students, students with teachers, teachers with teachers, and so forth.

## Students with Students

A community of students will develop naturally in a small group. Large groups automatically fragment into manageable smaller groups and therefore defeat the purpose of community building. We actively promoted a sense of community for our students by mixing grade levels and breaking down all notions of separation. We didn't offer classes exclusively for "accelerated learners." Our classes had mixed-ability groupings so that the students could learn how to include everyone in the learning adventure.

We didn't offer competitive team sports but instituted games where all students played. Using the "neighborhood model," we never kept the same teams, and chose team members on the spot. Our ball games were coed and everyone including staff played. We cheered on the timid ones and the little ones, and if someone couldn't run, we ran for him or her. These games promoted cooperation and teamwork but no identification with a certain group of people. The result of these combined efforts was that bullying and teasing did not occur. When the entire community is concerned about each other, there is a healthy pressure to do the right thing, as students take responsibility for each other.

Cigarette smoking among our students was a constant concern and every year we invited a speaker from the American Lung Association to give a talk. This speaker was a former smoker who had been a probation officer for teenagers for twenty-five years. He did a marvelous job presenting the hazards of smoking and used slides and video clips to show how the media were manipulating teens into believing smoking was cool:

A few days after one of our yearly anti-smoking sessions, Neil, a senior stood up at the assembly and made an impassioned plea to the whole school to stop smoking. He had tears in his eyes and said he didn't want to watch his friends killing themselves with this destructive activity. After this dramatic show of concern, a number of students actually did give up smoking and the attitude around school changed so that it became cool not to smoke.

In a community you learn how to listen, how to be loyal, how to express kindness, and how to stick up for others. With real concern for each other, students learn to value the qualities of the heart, mind, and soul as well as physical appearances or material possessions. The deepest need of every student is to be understood, respected, and valued for the unique person he or she is. By learning to live in community we attempted to fill this need and send our students into the world with confidence and compassion.

## Students and Teachers

One of the most important aspects of creating community between teachers and students is to eliminate as many barriers to communication as possible. At Mountain View we began by allowing the students to address us by our first names. We found that doing away with the formalities of "Mr.," "Mrs.," or "Miss" achieved the immediate result of increased accessibility and a sense of relaxation in the classroom.

By doing away with formalities, we were in essence giving the students permission to communicate more freely with us. It was an invitation to them to see us as part of their world, adults they could get to know and share aspects of their lives with that they wouldn't divulge to a "Mister" or a "Misses."

Students came to our homes to drop off papers, show off their cars, have a cup of tea, and talk about college. We organized garage sales, conducted play rehearsals, and baked cookies together in our homes. The English teacher brought her senior class home once a month for a "salon" atmosphere and critique of essays. We believe that the more teachers can do with kids after school, the more life they bring to the community.

## Teachers and Teachers

We promoted a community of cooperation among our teachers by allowing them a voice in the decision-making process. Our staff meetings were run by consensus and we gave every teacher a chance to discuss issues of concern at length until some plan of action was adopted.

Our teachers brought up all the problems they had with individual students and we worked as a group to create a coordinated plan to handle them. Instead of seeing individual problems with separate solutions handed down by the administration, we shared the issues

among the community of teachers and approached them from a consensus of agreement.

Each teacher invariably had a unique insight on each student and
as an integrated group we worked to come up with unique solutions
to problems:

John was a very intelligent and talkative young man with parents who held
postgraduate degrees in education. He once shared with one of his teachers
that he was an aspiring Bohemian poet. Having transferred into our school
from a public school that he found too confining, John had difficulty con-
taining his colorful expressiveness and highly charged energy. Coming into
a school environment that encouraged self-expression and inclusiveness was
nearly too much for him to handle. He immediately pulled out all the stops
and shifted into overdrive.

It became apparent at one of the staff meetings that John had pushed several of his teachers to the limit. His parents had been so thankful to us for
having provided a positive learning environment for their son that it was
going to be difficult to tell them he was turning out to be more that we could
handle.

The math teacher was outraged at his foul language and was threatening
to ban him from her class. The English teacher complained that John only
wanted to read the prose and poetry of the Beats and was constantly pull-
ing out Jack Kerouac's *On the Road* instead of the assigned literature. It was
only in history, where the class was constantly involved in hands-on projects
that called upon them to role-play and create "life experience" documenta-
ries with a video camera, that John really shined and didn't disrupt.

Instead of attempting to deal with his behavior one class at a time, we
structured the meeting with John's parents so that it wouldn't turn out to
be a negative tirade that offered one of two choices: "Your kid needs to clean
up his act or you can find him another school." We developed an integrated
approach to help John fit more comfortably into the school community.

On the day of the meeting we made it clear that John needed to alter his
behavior in his math class and show respect for the teacher's sensibilities. We
encouraged him to take a class in contemporary literature at the local community college in addition to his English class so he could study the literature he loved. He also received kudos for his active participation in his history class and was acknowledged for his creativity.

John and his parents came away from the meeting with plenty to think
about. Instead of being given an ultimatum, they were provided with options and alternatives and even encouragement. The integrated approach we
used helped John maintain his good feelings about the school. He hadn't
been rejected for his inappropriate behavior. He graduated and enrolled in
the university where his mother was a professor.

Another community-building activity was our yearly retreat, during which we invited all teachers to submit ideas for new programs and spent an entire day discussing them. If someone identified a need they thought the school could fill with a new class, an afterschool program, or a change in the way we dealt with discipline, we created a plan for working toward its implementation. We also demonstrated to each other creative teaching techniques we'd discovered that worked well in the classroom. These retreats were a community-building process and gave the staff a feeling of being included in deciding the direction the school would take in the future.

Another bridge of inclusiveness that we forged was having three teacher/administrators run the school instead of one person with ultimate say over all decisions. This allowed teachers the chance to approach one of the three administrators when they had issues they wanted to bring up. Invariably each teacher developed a rapport with the administrator they found easiest to approach. This ability to have a choice in who to talk to opened the communication and enhanced teacher-administrator relations.

## Students and Community at Large

School should extend beyond the campus and connect with the cultural environment of the surrounding community. Some of the ways we brought our students and the community together were through dances with other schools, entering the city's art contests, conducting classes at the coffee house, running on the bike trails, and teaching a curriculum based on the geographical region where we lived.

The major industries in our region were agriculture, tourism, and some aspects of the film business. We took our classes to visit a local orchardist, who talked with the students about his career as a citrus and avocado ranch manager. He also discussed the prospects for young people entering the field. Another class visited a film production company and interviewed a young entrepreneur, who explained how to enter the field, what the demands were, and the compensation. Being under thirty years old, he spoke their language while he showed them his editing equipment and some of the films he had produced.

In an organized class excursion our relations with the community members were productive, but when the teens were out in the neighborhood by themselves they could be strained. Sometimes the interactions with neighbors were problematic:

The school got a call from an irate neighbor who said that her mailbox had been opened up and vandalized. She was sure that it must have been one of our students, because they walked by her house every day. A mailbox was vandalized, a neighbor was angry, so we came together in assembly to address the issue.

We asked the students if they knew anything about the lady's mailbox. No one did, but the defenses started to fly: "How does she know that it was a student from our school—lots of kids walked down that street?" "Who is she to accuse us like that?" "Everyone hates teenagers."

We asked them, "What might happen to the school if we made enemies of the neighbors and were asked to move? Would we have to relocate out past the industrial estate?" Even if she assumed it was one of our students and it wasn't, how could we show her that we were good neighbors to have?

One student offered, "We could fix the mailbox, we could apologize." Others were indignant: "Why should we, when we didn't do it?" Another student offered that "even if one of us didn't do it, what about the neighbor's belief that we were responsible?"

We were pleased with the discussion, and it was concluded that we should tell the woman that the students didn't believe that one of them did it, but that they would be happy to fix the mailbox anyway. The staff was not convinced that one of our students hadn't vandalized the mailbox, but at least the entire school understood the repercussions from such an action.

High school students often have little awareness of their role in creating a supportive community. Without the high school facing issues such as these and including students in the solutions, teens can remain oblivious to their impact on the community at large. If the school doesn't take time to teach the value of mutual respect within the community, students do not learn about their interdependence. They leave school and go into the community without caring.

If we really want to have livable communities, we have to show kids how to live in community. Adolescents need an arena in which to try out their newly gained powers of understanding. Unfortunately, high schools, as they are today, isolate teens from society behind tall chain-link fences rather than integrate them into society.

## Students and the World

Our world has become very small and accessible, especially through the Internet. What we buy, do, and say affects the lives of people on the other side of the globe. This fact becomes especially clear when we understand how the environmental practices of a country are not contained by its borders. Ozone depletion from chlorofluorocarbon (CFC) emissions, overfishing of the world's oceans, and the fallout from the Chernobyl nuclear disaster are examples of how the practices of individual nations affect everyone on the planet.

For a small school we made a great effort to bring as much of the world into our school as we could. For example, we brought a filmmaker to share his adventures with the Wadabe tribe in Africa. We brought the Dalai Lama's official biographer to discuss the Tibetan tragedy. A black South African spoke about apartheid, and aboriginal grandmothers from Australia shared stories and songs. We had musicians play ragas from South India and offered an ethnic music class taught by a Tunisian. We enrolled international students from Japan, Brazil, and France.

Our environmental program exposed students to the crisis facing the planet's life support systems. The fact that we are at a critical time in the world when the future of the planet is at risk can inspire students to care for the earth. Since this is one of the major challenges for the upcoming generation, we felt an obligation to alert them. We called upon our students to expand their identities to include the planetary understanding that they will need to cope with the big problems on the horizon.

No matter what fields our teenagers go into, they need to carry a consciousness about the planet. Each needs an understanding of the closed-loop system in which we live. There's no place to throw anything away anymore. We have to grasp this concept or run the risk of destroying our food, water, and soil.

We encouraged students to approach these problems with a sense that the earth is their home and that the earth will sustain them if they protect the earth's systems. Being a resident of the planet, in community with all other residents, was the theme of our environmental program.

## COMMUNITY SOLVING PROBLEMS

There is no need to channel every school problem up the hierarchy to the top dog—the principal. What are we teaching when we do that? When the entire school community faces problems, everyone learns how to deal with challenges. Instead of proclamations coming from "on high," everyone owns the solution. Members of a community become more supportive of each other when they are aware of each other's vulnerability.

Being a safe place for all, Mountain View created an environment in which students were free to bring any issue to the staff. Teachers could come to any one of three administrators with a problem or an observation. Although some problems are too private and sensitive for the entire community to be included, a small group can effectively address many problems.

## A Problem-Solving Process

Sometimes the *process* of searching for solutions actually becomes the solution. We found this to be especially true with deep-seated and pervasive problems such as racial prejudice and intolerance that occasionally surfaced at our school. Rather than coming up with punitive directives from the administration to combat the problem or perhaps ignoring it altogether, we used a process for discussing the issue that pulled the school together as a community.

This process involved the entire school discussing the issue in a seminar fashion and then allowing the students to examine it in small groups so that they could formulate responses to share with the school as a whole:

About a month into the new school year a student told us that a group of boys were making racist remarks around the campus. According to this student, one of the boys even had an insignia on his ball cap making a disguised statement about white supremacy. A couple of teachers verified the reports and felt that it was serious enough to take action.

But what were we to do? We were aware of a degree of racial intolerance in the community at large, but were we willing to tolerate it in our school community? Should we call the students into the office and investigate, reprimand, suspend, or maybe even expel them?

Instead of taking punitive action we decided to have the entire school spend an afternoon considering the issue of racial intolerance. Prior to the seminar we formulated a list of questions dealing with prejudice. One of the questions was "How does it feel when someone judges you by the way you look?"

We divided the students into preselected discussion groups of five or six and assigned each group a teacher/facilitator. The group members were carefully selected so that each group would have a good gender mix and contain students with leadership qualities along with students who were more reluctant to participate. We also didn't place close friends together in the groups.

The groups were given an hour to discuss the list of questions and come up with responses to them. Each group went off to various classrooms or out on the lawn to record their comments and ideas. The students were encouraged to express any viewpoint or experience concerning racial intolerance. We then reconvened the groups and presented their thoughts and responses to the questions. This process helped link teachers with students and empowered the students to express their opinions, with the teachers acting in a facilitation capacity.

The process also generated a genuine heartfelt response from the various groups and helped them approach the issue as a community and see how individual responses contributed to the community. They were given the opportunity to speak freely and share their views without having to worry about possible consequences.

After the seminar the entire school came to the conclusion that prejudice was not cool and not appropriate. Exposing and talking about the issue may not have eliminated all feelings of racial intolerance, but it got everyone thinking about it and the reports of racial slurs on campus declined significantly. The ball cap with the suspect insignia was not seen on campus again.

This activity strengthened the concept of community by building confidence and trust between students and teachers. It showed that if a student was concerned about an issue and took it to the staff, it wouldn't go unattended. The process also kept the concerned student from being identified as a snitch who got everyone into trouble. It demonstrated to the students how a large group could function in a cohesive way, having tolerance for the opinions of every participant and allowing the process to become the solution.

## Cultural Diversity Efforts

The public high school in our town instituted a cultural diversity day to celebrate the various ethnic groups in the school district. It was a well-intentioned effort to generate understanding between the various cultures at a large high school. It was held after school in the gymnasium with speakers, music, and snacks. Ellen observed mainly Anglo kids, the class president, school officers, a few parents, many teachers, and some public officials in attendance. The student speakers were eloquently pleading for tolerance, in effect preaching to the choir.

We're not sure how much real progress is made with these large public events. It does bring the attention of the students and parents to the issue of diversity, but does it change any minds? When trying to teach tolerance we are up against subtle but strong unconscious ideas that children have learned as part of the family belief system. It takes more than a few well-spoken words to change prejudice.

When diverse students actually work side by side with one another to accomplish a shared goal, they usually drop the stereotypes and meet each other as individuals. The real breakthroughs come when teenagers of different ethnicity get to know each other and realize their common ground. A small school like Mountain View, which requires mutual respect and requires students to work together to accomplish something, can bring people together without preaching. Friendships can form or at least tolerance can be achieved through interaction.

## The Need for Limits

Even though inclusiveness encourages a sense of community at school, we also realize that limits need to be established and enforced. Without defining limits, a school community can be slowly eroded until it losses its capacity to nurture.

We found this to be especially true with drug use among our students. Over the years, we tried out various approaches to this dilemma. Our initial policy was zero tolerance for any type of drug use. But when we did gather enough evidence to dismiss a student for smoking pot in the park during the lunch hour, we came under criticism by one of the parents, who felt we needed to take a more sensitive approach to the issue. He suggested that we provide psychological assistance to our student drug users and educate them so that they could be persuaded to get off drugs.

We attempted to institute such a program and even sent one of our administrators to a workshop on how to set up a student assistance program in a school. But our program met with little success and the drug issue just seemed to keep growing and getting worse. Finally we realized that we just didn't have the expertise or personnel to handle teens on drugs. Our position was that a student on drugs at school would be learning very little, would be likely to spread the drug use to other students, and would therefore be a detriment to the school community.

In response to this we returned to our zero tolerance policy and began requesting that parents have their teens tested if we suspected that they were on drugs at school. If they tested positive, they were given a choice of both enrolling in a drug rehab program and losing the privilege of leaving the campus for up to a month; if they refused, we asked them to leave. This rule helped us begin to eliminate drug use from our campus.

We learned from this experience that maintaining limits is very important and that the limits have to be backed up with accountability and consequences or they won't be effective.

## SCHOOLS CREATE SOCIETY

When we look around at the symptoms of dysfunction in our society, we come to realize that we can't regard society as a role model for creating a healthy school community. The school should not reflect the crime, prejudice, and inequality that exist in society, but be a place where teenagers learn about what makes a truly healthy and functional community. In other words, we should be creating the ideal community at school:

Richard had never considered how much social institutions actually emerge out of school experiences until he listened to a talk by a Native American. At the time Richard was a member of a student activist group that had invited a Lakota elder named Ernie Longwalker to speak at their community college. Longwalker's speaking engagement coincided with college recruitment day, when all of the major colleges in the area had tables set up around the campus quad.

The student group didn't really know what Longwalker's talk was going to be about and perhaps he didn't either prior to his arrival that day. But what he said had a very big impact on Richard and the way he viewed the role of education in America. Longwalker began by reminding his audience of the terrible degradation taking place in the natural and social environment and how people seemed to be oblivious to the destruction of the very life-giving resources that they depended on for survival.

And then he really dropped the bomb. He laid the blame for this attitude squarely in the lap of the education system and said that if change didn't come soon in the way children were educated, the country's quality of life would be lost, perhaps irrevocably. He pointed out how the values taught in school had to change, that teachers had to begin to teach respect for the earth and people. In fact, the whole society had to transform its worldview from one of competition and mass consumption to one of sharing and cooperation.

Richard sat on the lawn riveted by Longwalker's words, and when he'd finished his talk Richard looked around the quad and was surprised to see that all the campus recruiters had folded up their tables and vanished. He hadn't even heard them leave. Later he wondered what had driven them away. Even though Longwalker's words seemed harsh, they made a big impression on the audience. Perhaps school officials need more wake-up calls like this to begin to understand the dilemma we are facing.

If we take a minute to think about it, we realize that society ultimately models itself after the school, not the other way around. The values and behaviors that children observe and imitate in the schoolyard are what they take with them out into the community. So if we really want to change society and correct its many dysfunctional aspects, we must first change the school to reflect the values and beliefs that we want to see flourish.

We believe that in order to eliminate violence, intolerance, and alienation, we must first remove these things from our schools. There are plenty of examples of how teens and young adults learn antisocial behavior at school and carry it with them into adulthood. One of the more publicized examples is the group of men who participated in the Committee to Reelect the President (CREEP) and orchestrated the Watergate break-in during the Nixon administration. Many of these highly educated people had been college friends and they learned their political dirty tricks during their years running student campaigns on the college campus.

If the purpose of the school is to produce citizens to compete in a cutthroat environment and win by whatever means possible, then the result will be a society where a sense of community is not honored and cooperation is considered a sign of weakness. But if the school's purpose is to recognize the benefits of collaboration and promote the notion that a strong sense of community will result in a healthy, sustainable society, then that's what the result will be. A society that invests time and energy in creating safe and nurturing schools that teach the lessons of compassion, equality, and tolerance will be investing in a safe and healthy future for all.

## Learning Democratic Decision Making

It's a well-accepted premise that a democracy can only remain healthy when a majority of its citizens participate in decision making. The continual erosion in the number of people who vote is a lament that we hear every time there's a national election. One of the major reasons for this apathy is the lack of training in decision making that is provided to the average high school student. We are not referring to a civics class where students are expected to learn the basics of the democratic system. What is needed is the true decision making in which students are given a voice and a vote in the operation of their schools.

How can we expect teens to want to participate in politics once they reach the magic age of eighteen if they've been deprived of genuine decision-making opportunities in school? In a school with hundreds or even thousands of students, providing bona fide decision-making opportunities is simply impossible. But in a school with a hundred or fewer students, real opportunities present themselves on a continual basis.

When a school is small enough to provide everyone with a chance to voice his or her opinion and have it included in decision making, then participation is encouraged. Teens have to know that their vote on any given issue counts, have to recognize that their participation in the democratic process translates into personal empowerment, have to understand the possible consequences of not participating.

## Mastering Skills of Community Responsibility

Teenagers are often looking for what the community can give them. Is there anything for them to do? Does the community have a teen center, a skate park, or a public swimming pool? Is there a place for them to hang out, play music, and engage in other activities they enjoy? And yet teens are very responsive to learning about their place in a community of grandparents, small children, and adults. They readily accept the responsibility for their role once they have been accepted into the larger community.

We once asked our students, "What is your biggest concern about our town?" and were surprised at the candid response to our question. It was unanimous. The most disturbing thing for them was the "cheezy" music coming out of the post office tower every hour on the hour. The Civic Association had installed a bell chime that played 1940s and 1950s show tunes and love songs to the downtown shoppers every hour. Next to the post office tower was a lovely park where the teens gathered and socialized. The teens could not stand the music. "Couldn't something be done?" Every hour they had to listen to this "gawdawful stuff."

This was an excellent opportunity for the teens to look beyond their self-interest and see themselves as part of the community at large. At the end of a lively discussion, they concluded that they were a relatively small voice in relation to the entire population of the town. Other citizens would outnumber their wishes. Parents and retired people probably enjoyed it and children probably didn't mind the tunes either.

So what could they do? Various teens made some interesting proposals, but none that was acceptable to the whole group. They were not interested in raising money to purchase other music. They didn't feel that they had a strong enough claim on the "ear space" to take the issue to local government. It was concluded that they would not like the music *ever,* but that they would tolerate the hourly intrusions into their sound environment for the sake of the community as a whole. It was a valuable exercise in living in the larger community.

Our students fed the homeless, adopted a beach to clean up, and volunteered at the local hospital. Through these kinds of activities, they learned of the needs of the community and how we are responsible for each other. Their own musical taste paled in significance as one of the issues the larger community faced.

In our town the city government was very responsive to the voice of youth. A high school student sat on the parks and recreation commission and a youth commission was formed. Youth comments were warmly welcomed at the city council meetings. Every community could benefit from giving the youth in their community a responsible voice in city affairs.

Parents can be instrumental in requesting this kind of youth participation. After all, the parents are the politicians' constituents, and meeting the needs of youth is a viable and popular political issue.

## Learning Collaborative Action

There were many opportunities for our students to learn about collaborative action in order to achieve a successful result. We tirelessly promoted teamwork in areas like organizing school dances, camping trips, and even the graduation ceremony.

In civics class the students had two major opportunities each year to practice collaborative action. The first of these activities was a political topic that they worked together to address and the second was an entrepreneurial project:

After brainstorming ideas for the year's civics class business, the students decided they wanted to open a one-day coffeehouse that offered a variety of beverages, a relaxing and casual atmosphere, and music and entertainment. Right from the start the whole class agreed upon every decision that was made on the project.

During this entrepreneurial unit they learned all about the economics of business ownership and the advantages and disadvantages of sole proprietorship, partnerships, and corporations. They learned about tax laws, interest rates, prime locations, budgeting, and the difference between net and gross revenues.

The teacher could tell this was going to be an interesting project when they decided to call their coffeehouse "The Tibetan House of Rest." Because they were completely in charge of the project, he allowed them to run with it and see where they would end up. It was fascinating to watch the process of collaboration once they decided upon their goal. Someone was appointed to handle publicity, someone else took care of rounding up appropriate decorations that matched the exotic theme. One group organized the necessary coffee-making equipment and another supplied the music.

The students worked together on the day of the event to welcome their customers—fellow students, parents, and friends—provide good service, and enhance the atmosphere of an avant-garde coffeehouse with pillows, tapestries, and appropriate Eastern music. Their project succeeded beyond all expectations. They learned basic business practices and each shared in the profit that was earned. Everyone had a good time and they experienced the success of collaborative action without any help from an adult.

## Change Is Natural

Most private high schools operate on a reputation based on a tradition or a style of education that has set them apart from others. Each campus seems to have a certain culture: academic achievement, a rugged outdoor character-building program, a particular religious upbringing, or artistic excellence. These schools look for a certain student profile to meet the mold they have created. When students arrive on campus, they are given a set of expectations, codes of behavior, academic standards, and social behaviors to adopt and conform to. Schools often maintain these traditions for generations.

Because our school was small and student-centered, it allowed us flexibility to adapt to the students rather than impose a rigid structure. What was amazing was that every year the structure changed. We were constantly altering our curriculum (beyond the basics) in response to what the teachers and the students identified as the proper direction for the school, and we continually solicited input from them in order to respond to their goals and aspirations.

We shouldn't take for granted that we know what's best for teenagers. They need to be acknowledged and encouraged to provide input about the kinds of things they would like to learn. We saw the school as an ever evolving and changing offering. Our job as administrators was to facilitate learning, creativity, and growth and to accommodate the changes in attitudes and desires among the student body and teachers.

When we received sufficient input from the students about some class or program they wanted, we took this information into our teacher/staff retreat and worked to formulate a plan for implementing it. Our basic rule in this regard was that if we had at least three students interested in a class, we would do our best to offer it.

Mountain View students were always interested in drama, so we offered a drama class that focused on improvisation. After the second year of this program the students really wanted to do a full-fledged play to be performed in the community theater in our town. So we arranged to hire a drama teacher who had experience with teenage productions. By this time nearly the entire school was enrolled in the drama program and they chose an ensemble play called *Voices from the High School* in which pairs of students performed vignettes that were tied together by a common theme. They worked very hard to present a polished performance and the play drew a packed house.

The students came away from this experience feeling enormously accomplished because they had conceived of an idea for a class, requested that we implement it, and, when it became a successful reality, were able to claim total ownership of it.

## TWENTY QUESTIONS FOR PARENTS

1. Do you know if your teenager is enjoying a supportive educational community?

2. Are you satisfied with the values of your teenager's peer group?

3. Is your teenager confident about his or her attractiveness and sexual identity?

4. Does your teenager feel like he or she belongs to a loosely knit group of friends and acquaintances?

5. Are you aware of a culture of cliques at your teen's school and how it impacts your teen's life?

6. Is inclusiveness a value your teenager learns at home?

7. What activities at your teen's school are consciously intended to promote community building, such as mixed-ability groupings, cooperative games, and the like?

8. Does your teen ever meet with teachers outside of the classroom?

9. Do you know if teachers at your child's school have a chance to collaborate and coordinate their efforts with other teachers?

10. Does your teenager participate in a variety of organized activities in the community generated by the school?

11. Is your teenager's view of the world limited and parochial or broad and international?

12. How are "problems" handled at your student's high school: by private reprimands, dismissals, detentions, and subsequent rumors or does the school include students in the solutions?

13. Is your student aware of the rules or limits at the school and confident that consequences will ensue if rules are broken?

14. When you observe your local high school, do you see the students demonstrating values for a positive future for society?

15. Does your child have authentic decision-making opportunities at the local high school?

16. Does your teen express a sense of responsibility for the quality of life in your town or city?

17. Does your teenager engage in any community service activities or youth politics?

18. Does your student collaborate with other students on group projects for a class or for a school activity?

19. Is your local high school able to be flexible in its classes on extracurricular activities to meet the needs of the student community?

20. Do you feel that your child is learning to participate in the many levels of community by attending high school?

## CHAPTER EIGHT

# Parents Have Choices

Rick's mother contacted us midway through his tenth-grade year. Hers was a familiar story, with a son who was bright and energetic but struggling to make passing grades at the local public high school. Rick had also been experiencing spells of gloom and depression and his doctor had recommended medication.

After six months at our school it was hard to imagine how Rick could have been nearly failing. He was an exceptionally gifted and enthusiastic learner. He thrived in the gentle and supportive atmosphere at Mountain View, where we were all on a first-name basis. Although he still encountered some difficulty getting his homework turned in, his exceptional linguistic and analytical skills made him shine. His wild impulses and flashy creativity found an appreciative audience and his self-esteem improved immeasurably.

After graduation Rick was accepted with a full scholarship to a prestigious college in Massachusetts. He earned high grades and received a sponsorship to study abroad during his final two years. Rick told us he never would have found his life path without the support of our school. Before enrolling at Mountain View he never even considered college. Our school, with its small classes, supportive environment, and family atmosphere, gave him the confidence he needed to succeed in higher education.

If frustration and anxiety have become your normal reaction to your child's experience at school and you've done all you can to address the problems but to no avail, perhaps it is time to find another school. We encourage parents to look at all the options available and find the school that is the best fit for their child. This chapter will explore the many options available and provide help in what to look for.

## PUBLIC SCHOOLS OR PRIVATE SCHOOLS?

Are your children happy to go to school each day? Are they getting satisfactory grades, having a healthy social life, and interested in what they are learning? If not, then it is important for you to do something!

Parents should thoroughly investigate the schools their children attend. We shouldn't just pack our kids off to school with the assumption that everything is okay. Teenagers are not always forthcoming when we ask them things like, "How's it going at school?" It may take some aggressive sleuthing for you to determine the answers to the questions above. This section will identify what to look for.

### Public Schools

Parents often see education as a limited choice between public and private schools. We feel that many assumptions about public and private education are misleading and that the individual school is what needs scrutiny. Although we oppose large impersonal institutions, we have found some outstanding public schools and private schools as well as poor-quality schools in both categories.

We applaud the efforts and intent of the public school system. There is no lack of devotion in most public schools. Individual teachers and administrators are making immense efforts for the nation's students. It is the way that most of these schools are structured that creates the huge problems and serious concerns that are addressed throughout this book.

Parents ultimately hold the reins on the public schools system because their tax money supports the system. Parents can push for reductions in class size, voice concerns about building designs when a new school is proposed for their district, register a dissatisfaction with the pressure to teach to the test, and ask that teachers be given more latitude to innovate in their classrooms. Parents can also work with a high school to encourage a climate of cooperation and inclusion to alleviate the devastating effects of bullying, shunning, and cliques.

People who are committed to public education should be willing to consider any workable option. A well-informed parent who is adamant about having a top-quality high school in the community can be a great boon. Schools and parents can work together to create the ideal educational environment.

We encourage parents to begin to get involved by carefully investigating what their children face in school each day. You may wish to schedule a daylong visit to sit in on your student's classes. The following is a checklist of what to look for when scrutinizing a school:

1. *Classroom size* of up to forty students assumes that the learning will be accomplished through the lecture format. Very little personal attention is possible. Crowd control, attendance rules, and threats of poor grades keeps order. What is the current size of your student's classes?

Thirty-five students or over
Twenty to thirty-four students
Under twenty students

2. What impact is class size having on learning? Is your student *actively engaged* in the learning process? What is the level of attentiveness in the class?

Students passively listen to the teacher for the entire class
Students are occasionally involved in hands-on learning activities
Students are continually involved in a variety of learning activities that call
    upon them to discuss, analyze, and implement

3. The *large institutional design* of most high school buildings is not conducive to learning. Is your student's campus scaled to the human dimension and incorporated into the natural environment? Do students show respect for the physical campus? Rate the campus quality:

Cold, impersonal, neglected
Standard construction with efforts to beautify
Inviting campus integrated into the natural surroundings

4. A *classroom design* that invites student discussion and participation is one that has students facing one another rather than students looking at others' backs. Classrooms that respect students' learning are also clean and attractive. How are the classrooms in your student's school set up?

Rows facing a blackboard, poor ventilation, dilapidated furnishings

Rows facing blackboard in a clean attractive room

Seating around a table in a clean attractive room

5. A *curriculum strictly coordinated* with testing takes spontaneity and creativity away from teachers. The soul of teaching is missing. A parent can observe teacher enthusiasm and the level of interaction with students, but curriculum content and the school's adherence to it will be impossible to determine in one visit. Questioning the administration or the teachers may yield answers. During the initial visit, look for the following:

Teacher is intent on covering the material, unresponsive to student interest in it

Teacher is occasionally breaks the routine to engage with students

Teacher is deeply engaged with student thought processes and responses to curriculum

6. *Teacher quality* is often the most obvious for parents to determine in a school visit. A teacher who loves his or her job and enjoys the students creates a classroom atmosphere that is alive and ripe for learning. Record your observations:

Teacher is lifeless, annoyed with students, tired of the subject

Teacher is having a few high points but generally following a routine

Teacher is enjoying the class, excited about the subject, and engaging the students in learning

7. Determining the *quality of the student body* is often more challenging for parents. Rather than looking at their presentation, such as clothes and hairstyles, we advise parents to observe whether kids make eye contact, are genuinely polite, and are at ease and bright-eyed in their learning environment.

Students are sullen, plodding, and unresponsive

A few students look sparkling and accomplished, most are disengaged

All students on campus are charged with the exhilaration of being in the right learning environment for them

8. Since *high school is mandatory* in the state of California to age sixteen, most public schools are obligated to enroll every student who

registers. Some private schools accept every applicant due to economic necessity. The result is that many of the students don't want to be where they are and react through rebellion and resistance. Some school districts provide alternative schools that offer educational options for students who don't fit the norm. Parents should know what options or alternatives the school provides:

Is the school compelled to accept every applicant?

Would many students rather not be in the school but are there because the school district offers no alternative?

Does every student want to be in that particular educational environment?

9. What is the *social climate* on the campus outside the classroom? Is the campus alive with friendly greetings, simply impersonal, or do you sense a hostility between students? Do you observe cliques?

Students are bunched up into tight groups of lookalikes with a few loners by themselves

Most students look content, with a few looking lost

Students are intermingling with each other in a relaxed and flowing way

After experiencing the classroom and scrutinizing its quality, our advice is to find out about programs at your high school that may enrich your child. As this chapter points out, public schools are capable of creating innovative programs to respond to the public disaffection with "schooling as usual." Often there are innovations in the local public high school that may not be known to parents. Here is an example of an innovation that was linked to the marketplace excerpted from an article called "Why These Schools Work" by Hedrick Smith that appeared on page 12 in *Parade Magazine* on January 4, 1998:

In Oakland, California, public high schools were in terrible shape in 1985. A third of the students entering high school were not graduating, and those who were earning diplomas were getting only a ninth-grade education. The school district decided to do something, opting to try a career academy—a school within a school that offered courses in a specific field linked to paid internships.

At Oakland Technical High School, rated as the city's worst, one teacher, Patricia Clark, saw healthcare as a field with great potential. Clark created the Health and Biosciences Academy, the first and still the largest of

Oakland's twenty-eight career academies. While it takes top students, its focus is on chronic underachievers like Kennard Davis, who grew up in tough West Oakland and was barely passing. The academy changed that. "It's a tremendous turn-on," Davis says. "You get to actually do and see for yourself."

Course standards are tough, but a close-knit atmosphere makes students feel that teachers care. A big motivator is the prospect of paid summer internships for those with C+ or better averages, where students get hands-on experience working with professionals. In the graduating class of 1997, eighty-seven of ninety-three Health and Biosciences Academy students went on to college.

## Private Schools

When parents decide to look beyond the local public school to the private sector, the first objection for many is that the private schools are too expensive. Although the cost of tuition and books is a challenge for many families, few private schools make a profit. But most private schools have sizable scholarship programs through gifts or endowments. Parents should not let cost keep them from finding the right school for their children. If you find the right school for your child and it is too expensive, apply for a partial or full scholarship.

Here are the stories of two of the students who came to our school on scholarships.

Sam was one of our most outstanding students. He felt he could get better grades and learn more in a smaller school, so he arranged for his own interview at Mountain View. He was an average student at the public high school who became a standout in our more personalized environment.

Sam's parents owned a small pizza parlor and had eleven children and couldn't afford tuition. We offered him a partial scholarship and he worked part time to pay the balance. He was always on time with his monthly payment and graduated with a very high grade point average. Sam went on to the local university, where he studied to be a history teacher.

Leona's mother was a dance instructor/choreographer and led a community dance company. Her schedule was irregular and her work was sporadic. She wanted Leona to be in a caring school environment where she would feel more at home. Leona also wanted to arrange her schedule so that she could continue to teach gymnastics to young children.

Leona was an average student who was struggling to maintain interest in school. She was also an outstanding gymnast who had won a state championship. We worked out a tuition that the pair could manage and were also able to arrange a schedule that supported Leona's continued success in gymnastics. Leona thrived in the small classes, raised her grade point average, and took a full-time job teaching gymnastics after graduation. She also attended community college at night.

Private schools are not necessarily better than public schools. Every kind of criticism leveled at public schools can be applied equally to private schools. Just because a school is prestigious or expensive does not mean it is the right school for your child. We recommend using the checklist supplied above in the section titled "Public Schools" on every school, but not to be intimidated by cost.

Although you may not choose the private school route for your child, some offer unique programs for students who need to be actively involved in their education. Here's an example:

Midland School, a rustic college preparatory boarding school, is nestled on nearly three thousand acres of oak-studded rolling hills in the Santa Ynez Valley in central California. Although Midland has demanding academic standards and a rigorous curriculum, it is the self-sufficiency of the students that sets it apart. Wood-burning stoves heat the sixty wooden buildings. Students chop wood, prepare meals, tend horses, and attend to every other chore on campus—there is no maintenance staff. The idea is that students leave Midland knowing they can take care of themselves.

## OTHER CHOICES

Parents have many choices other than public school or the traditional private school. With so many teenagers balking at the education system and the continued policy of mandatory education to year twelve, alternatives have been initiated to fill the gap. Public school districts and innovative entrepreneurs are starting successful alternative schools. The public system is even being challenged in some cities by private donors who have offered to fund private school for thousands of poor children. We are living in a climate of choice for high school education.

### Alternative Schools

Many public school districts find that if they provide an alternative to the high school, it solves myriad problems. Students who are reluctant to attend a full day at the high school will often fulfill their educational requirement if given an alternative option. Students who are falling through the cracks, students with truancy or behavior problems, students who need personalized attention all can have their needs met in a good alternative school.

A parent may wonder what an alternative school really is. Although we will provide examples and descriptions in this section, each alternative school is unique and should be looked at on its own merits. Bill Hammond, instructional coordinator for alternative education with the DeKalb County, Georgia, school system, described alternative schools in an article titled: "Ask an Expert: What Is Philosophy of Alternative Education":

Alternative education programs provide students with a number of opportunities to succeed by . . . drawing on the preferred learning styles for the students. Assignments and instruction use a variety of methods to allow students and teachers to explore subject content through technology, fluid and flexible grouping patterns, extended times for instructional investigation, use for dual text and expanded resources in the classroom, and other selected techniques. . . . In some instances the student's self-esteem and confidence must be built up to the point that he or she believes in himself or herself.

A parent might ask what a school like this looks like and how the goals enumerated by Dr. Hammond are achieved. Ellen describes how it worked in an alternative high school called "Chaparral," which she frequently visited. This school provides an escape valve for a large public school. Many students are able to earn a diploma that otherwise would be out of reach.

Chaparral has an enrollment of under two hundred students and its own principal. The classrooms are in an extension of the school district administrative offices and have a normal institutional look. What is strikingly different is the casual attitude of the students, who are frequently sitting around tables and working independently or talking with each other rather than listening to a lecture. The teacher is moving around, answering questions, helping with problems, and engaging in conversations with individual students or small groups. These skilled teachers are the most empathetic and dedicated whom Ellen ever observed.

Classes are held only in the morning and consist of units that are self-taught and written work that is graded by teachers. Help is available for any subject. In order to earn credits for graduation, a number of units have to be completed. Students work at their own pace.

The students are a little rough around the edges and not all of them look happy to be there. But they seem to be committed to the task at hand and appreciative of the personal attention from the teachers. They are not in open rebellion, which is in evidence on many high school campuses. But the most significant observation is that the students approach the work with the attitude that they are capable of success. They understand the task and its consequences and are digging in to complete the work.

Alternative schools are usually small, often designed by the people who teach in them, and are created so that students have choices. Personal attention and less bureaucracy enable a sense of community to develop. Some alternative schools offer drop-in study centers, which provide assistance for any student upon request, and others offer enrichment programs for gifted students.

The primary mission of the Columbus Alternative High School, in Ohio is to prepare all students for formal postsecondary education. Students achieve this goal through community involvement and a strong academic program. It fosters positive growth in social behaviors and attitudes and encourages natural curiosity, which makes learning a lifelong choice. Columbus is a public magnet school designed to serve academically oriented students with a rich offering in the fine and performing arts. Although the school has no sports, the students have a big interest in chess; they take part in a popular chess club and hold chess tournaments.

Every school district has unique needs. The following is a description of an alternative school that was responsive to the needs of local industry:

Berkeley Alternative School is in proximity to the University of California at Berkeley. In describing the school, one member of the UC Berkeley Parents Network says, "This is not a 'continuation high,' it is an exciting program that integrates high academic standards with career paths, allowing the student to prepare for college and/or a career at the same time. The classes are small, the classrooms large and well quipped, and the campus is clean, safe, and pleasant."

Berkeley Alternative High School provides a calm, safe, and supportive learning environment for two hundred students with a project-based curriculum. The principal says, "We want to meet the needs of a changing student population, by partnering with the industries of health care, information technology, and hospitality and tourism."

## Charter Schools

The following definition of charter schools is from the Charter Schools Development Center in California:

Charter schools are a new form of public school designed to spur innovation in both individual schools and in general. Started by teachers, principals, parents and community groups, charter schools are freed from most of the restrictive laws that govern traditional public schools. In return for this freedom, charter schools are held more accountable for student success. Funded like other public schools, they operate under five year charter contracts that may be renewed if the school meets its performance goals. California's 300-plus charter schools serve a diverse range of students and often feature alternative or unique instructional programs.

When a group of parents gets serious about an alternative to the traditional public school, they have the option of starting a charter school. Usually it takes at least one person who makes it his or her life to get a charter off the ground. It requires much preparation and hoop-jumping, such as gaining the approval of the school district, but the results can be heartening. The obvious benefit of a charter school is that the funding is dependable, since it comes from the state in the form of a set amount for each student. While receiving funding, the charter school is relatively free of the burdensome regulations of public education.

Each charter school defines its own philosophy and implements it independently. One group attempting to form Doniphan Oaks Charter School in Ojai, California, put forth the following objectives:

- A small school with small class sizes
- Hands-on, project-based lessons
- An individualized, student-centered approach
- An outdoor environmental science program
- An integrated visual and performing arts program
- Collaborative teaching and learning
- More parent involvement

In Washington, Cesar Chavez Public Charter High School for Public Policy started with the promise that with a strong curriculum it would prepare students for college.

Charter schools are housed in strip malls, old grade schools, and larger school buildings as schools within schools. Parochial schools are even applying for public charter school status in some states, with religion being taught after hours. Charter schools come in many shapes and packages.

Horizons Community High School in Michigan has been in operation for over twenty years. It is an alternative charter high school with the motto "Teaching is more about listening than talking and learning is more about talking than listening." Although the student body has around two hundred members, every student is part of a smaller group with a teacher. Another unique feature is that students actually interview other students seeking admission.

## Home Schools

According to the most recent U.S. Census figures, at least 850,000 students were learning at home in 1999. But Rebecca Carroll's article "Back to School: More Families Opting to Home School Their Children" quoted Brian Ray, president of the National Home Education Research Institute, who said the federal figures are low. Ray believes that the number is actually twice that and growing because some home schooled students don't report themselves. In the past twenty years as the numbers have grown, home schooling has come under closer and closer scrutiny. The verdict is in on home schooling and it is very positive. From every indication, children who are schooled at home are excelling. The average home schooled student's SAT score is 1100, which is 80 points higher than the average score for the general population.

Monica and her sister were taught at home until they reached high school age. They were two beautiful, musically talented, and academically bright girls who'd had the full attention of their gifted mother all of their lives. The mother had always taken her cues from the girls' interests. The family unit had created a rich learning environment for them even though they followed no formal educational structure. But when the girls reached high school age, they wanted more of a social life than home schooling could provide.

Although they excelled academically and had no qualms about touting their achievements, it was the social life at school that compelled them. They mixed and mingled like butterflies. The focus of their lives shifted from home to campus. It was interesting to watch them consider the points of view of other students that they obviously had not been introduced to at home. They suffered disappointments and triumphs in friendships and romances and matured through it all.

These girls possessed tremendous scholastic confidence, and by being on a high school campus they acquired timely social skills that helped them adapt to the Ivy League colleges they were admitted to after graduation.

We believe that learning at home should not stretch students beyond what they can do on their own. We question whether a student can learn a subject such as geometry without a teacher. We are concerned that teenagers studying at home miss the opportunity to form mentoring relationships with adults outside of the family. But the most serious concern is that teens will miss the time in their lives when they need to learn to socialize with their peers.

The following list of "developmental tasks" is from the American Academy of Child and Adolescent Development. It states that in early adolescence, the developmental tasks are: having close friendships, finding new people to love in addition to parents, being influenced by peer group interests and clothing styles, having same-sex friends and group activities, and worrying about being normal. In middle adolescence the tasks are: accommodating a lowered opinion of parents, making new friends, and strongly emphasizing the new peer group. In late adolescence, that is, between ages seventeen and nineteen, the developmental tasks include: developing self-reliance, developing greater concern for others, and developing serious relationships.

These developmental tasks seem highly problematic for students who stay at home with their parent as the teacher until they are seventeen or eighteen. Although high school home schooling looks like a recipe for disaster, it is becoming more popular. One group reports that it "saved them from having to attend public school." We would like to see more options become available for students who do not thrive in public high schools, but we feel that home schooling is short-changing our teens.

### Schools Online

An online school is essentially schooling by computer. The course content, tests, and assignments are delivered through the computer. A teacher is available through e-mail for questions and to grade assignments and tests.

The benefits that online programs claim are that students can learn at their own pace, learning is flexible, students don't get bored, and they receive quick feedback by e-mail. Many online programs are state-run and offer accredited courses to supplement on-campus classes. Some are publicly funded and run by universities, and others are costly programs sold by online business ventures.

Online education suffers from the same social isolation that home schooling does. Can a parent provide mentoring adults and a circle of friends to develop social skills if a teenager is not going to school? On the other hand, if a student is in a school situation where he or she is fearful and therefore can't learn, the safety provided by good-quality online learning can be a godsend. But we feel that with all that is lacking with online schooling and because of the many other options available, it should only be a last resort for parents.

Cyber School is an example of an online high school whose motto is "Real teachers, real students, no walls." Cyber School is a public school organization with state-certified teachers that helps high schools provide a wide-ranging curriculum. If a school is too small to offer a specialized class, it can use the services of Cyber School to offer the class online.

In conclusion, we feel that school attendance is important for teenagers, so they can learn the habits of successful living. Whether students end up working as a scientist in a research lab or at the fast food restaurant, they have to get to work on time, wear the right clothes, and have lunch money. Many of these skills are acquired just by attending school.

In our years at Mountain View, there was always a kid at school who had no money, brought no food, and was "starving." One girl wore skimpy clothes and wanted to sit by the heater all winter. There were others who had no paper or pens. Borrowing became a way of life, a habit that needed to be broken before it became too entrenched. If students don't get these skills in high school, when will they learn them?

In our life skills class we taught students how to open a checking account. We prepared them for the potential pitfalls of their first credit card, which they would surely be offered once they enrolled in college. We explained how credit cards become the downfall for many college students when they run up a huge debts without any means to pay them off.

The students who wanted to leave home the minute they graduated learned the costs of renting an apartment. They created a budget for food, telephone, electricity, and first and last month's rent. They added up the cost of just starting out on their own. Then they looked at what kind of income they would need. After completing this assignment, 99 percent of them decided they would stay at home for a while.

## NEW EDUCATORS OFFER MORE CHOICES

### Entrepreneurs

Education is the second largest sector in the economy next to healthcare. It is a $700-plus billion a year industry. Business is seeing a hot new opportunity because of the widespread dissatisfaction with the current educational offering. Entrepreneurs have studied the inefficiencies, cost inflation, and inequity and think they can do a better job. Entrepreneurs from the private sector are playing a big role in public school as well starting private alternatives in the following ways:

- *Supplying extra instruction.* Private companies contract with public schools to provide such afterschool programs as tutoring, English as a second language, and special needs instruction.
- *Managing whole schools.* Educational management organizations (EMOs) operate like health management organizations (HMOs) to bring "efficiency" to the education sector and address the "bottom line," so far with mixed results.
- *Contracting with public schools to provide alternative high schools.* Private companies own and run alternative high schools funded by the public school system (twenty-two schools in Chicago and thirty-one in Milwaukee alone).

Eric Schwartz is the cofounder and president of Citizen Schools in Boston. He came from a career in journalism and political campaign management and includes himself in what he sees as a rise in "social entrepreneurism." An article in the *Christian Science Monitor* titled "Social Entrepreneurs Eagerly Move Forward," by Marjorie Coeyman, quotes Schwartz: "A lot of people are looking for meaning and are realizing that in the non-profit field you can be an entrepreneur, have the thrill of building something and dealing with big issues, but still be helping young people and making the community a better place to live."

Some of these entrepreneurs are coming straight out of college or graduate school, but others are career changers, people who have excelled in other lines of work but feel that they can make a contribution in education. Parents may want to investigate the legal structure of whatever educational option they choose. There are many motives for operating a school.

The Weil Tennis Academy is a for-profit boarding high school with a standard academic curriculum. What makes it exceptional is the intensive tennis training its students receive. Located next to a tennis club in a town with a famous amateur tennis tournament, the academy is a business that attracts the young tennis hopefuls.

### Institutions

High schools that are attached to institutions are opening in some unexpected places—in libraries, in churches, and in universities (some have attached pilot high schools to demonstrate educational innovations). This trend will continue as the large impersonal high schools fall out of favor.

## STARTING A SCHOOL

Starting a school may seem like a daunting task and is certainly not something to take on with less than a full commitment. Schools come in many shapes and sizes and some of the best schools in the nation started out with one person who had a vision.

Mountain View High School evolved out of an effort by a group of parents to provide a safe and nurturing educational environment for their children. They started off with a home schooling program and when their kids reached high school age they decided to bring them together with other teens in a classroom environment so that they could work and study together in a group and interact socially. Gradually the school expanded until it was a full-fledged nonprofit corporation with a beautiful facility, caring teachers, and a mission of drawing out the genius of every child.

### Prepare a Mission Statement

It is important when launching any endeavor that everyone involved is clear about the purpose. Having a clear mission statement that can be expressed in one succinct sentence or paragraph is vital for healthy beginnings. With a very simple statement of purpose or mission, potential confusion and conflict among those involved can be avoided. There is nothing worse when beginning an organization than a lack of clarity.

Along with a mission statement, the founders of a school should also be clear about what kinds of students would best suit the school. If the intent is to exclude no one who wishes to enroll, this is fine as long as everyone is in agreement and understands what it entails.

We are not referring to discrimination based on gender, national, or ethnic origins, which is illegal if the school is to be a tax-exempt nonprofit corporation. What we are talking about are the qualities that one looks for to determine how well students will interact with each other and what their aims and goals are. Are they sincerely interested in learning and contributing to a healthy school environment or are they merely looking for a place to get by on minimum effort? Sometimes students who come into a school with a counterproductive attitude can be persuaded to change and adapt to the program. But if too many in the school don't support goals of cooperation and focused learning, a school can fragment and self-destruct. Thus a statement about expectations concerning students is vital to the successful startup of a school.

### Find a Facility

Mountain View High School had its origins in the social hall of an Episcopalian church. As the student body grew, the church cooperated by providing a small office and then allowed the school to use two of its Sunday-school rooms. At it most active, Mountain View was using four rooms for classes and also using the office to occasionally tutor individual students.

We worked hard to maintain cordial relations with the church congregation and staff and provided the church with much needed income in the form of rent. We also routinely cleaned the facility and never complained when we were required to clean up messes made by other groups.

One of the most important things to consider when thinking about a facility for a school is its atmosphere and ambiance. A quite atmosphere within a naturally beautiful setting is the ideal, but may not always be attainable or feasible. Sometimes compromises must be made.

As we mentioned earlier, church facilities are one of the most likely candidates for schools. The schedules of church and school rarely conflicted in the case of Mountain View, and the layout of buildings, with a large lawn and trees surrounding them, created a pleasant and educationally conducive atmosphere. The fact that the church was located on a quiet street with a low volume of traffic also contributed to the positive climate. Civic buildings such as community centers and park and recreation facilities are also possibilities that should be considered. Other options include American Legion halls, Masonic lodges, summer camps, and recreation halls.

One potential pitfall is opting to purchase a facility for a school. Even a well-established school faces the constant challenge of balancing income with expenses. Unless a school has built up a substantial endowment to cover mortgage payments, a fledgling school is better off as a tenant rather than as a landlord.

We know of one successful school that had been in operation for ten years and decided to launch a fundraising campaign to purchase its own facility. The campaign took a tremendous amount of energy away from the function of the school itself. Even though the staff and parents were able to raise enough money for a down payment, being strapped with large monthly mortgage payments nearly bankrupted the school. They were forced to move back to their original facility and forfeited their down payment.

## Create a Nonprofit

The obvious advantage of applying for nonprofit status for a school is that it exempts the school from paying federal corporation taxes. The school staff's salaries are still taxed by the normal rules of the Internal Revenue Service, but the school itself is relieved of any business tax burden. Another advantage to having nonprofit status is the ability to apply for grants from corporations, foundations, and the federal government. Contributions from individual donors are tax-deductible.

The process of applying for nonprofit status can also help focus the mission and potential size of the school. The application process requires that a mission statement be submitted along with a projected budget for the first three years of operation. This requirement serves to bring the vision of the school into focus and helps potential applicants discover how serious they are about actually starting a school.

While the application process is time-consuming, it can be made easier with a publication called the *Non-Profit Corporation Handbook*. This is an excellent guide to the process and even provides most of the forms needed to complete the application.

## Families and Teachers

A core group of families and teachers needs to be established early in the process. When working through all of the challenges any new enterprise faces, the group will gain strength by being able to rally around a cohesive purpose. Our school kept the family participation interactive and fun, and this kept the parents involved. Parents made significant contributions not only in fundraising but also in regard to the curriculum, field trips, graduation ceremonies, and membership on the board of directors.

Schools need to gain new enrollments every year to keep afloat. Each year we advertised the school and prepared press releases about our students' accomplishments. But the vast majority of the families who found their way to our school came by word of mouth. When students and parents were happy with the school they told their friends and word got around.

## Call on Us If You Need Help

One of the dreams of the administrators of Mountain View High School has been to share the results of our experiment with other educators and parents. We want to share our experience because of the positive impact our school had on the lives of teens. We are committed to helping any group who desire to form an alternative school and could benefit from our experience. Please feel free to write to us:

Ellen Hall and Richard Handley
PMB Box 421
402 West Ojai Ave., Suite 101
Ojai, California 93023

# Bibliography

## PREFACE

Bauman, Kurt J. *Homeschooling in the United States: Trends and Characteristics*. Washington, D.C.: Bureau of the Census Population Division. www.census.gov/population/www/documentation/twps0053.html#data, 2001.

California State University Institute of Education Reform, Charter Schools Development Center. *National Statistics Overview, The National Charter School Directory*. Sacramento, CA: Center for Education Reform, California State University. www.uscharterschools.org/pub/uscs, 2003.

Pierson, David. "State Warns Parents of Home School Edict." *Los Angeles Times*. October 10, 2002, p. B1.


## CHAPTER 1

Berktold, Jennifer, Sonya Geis, Phillip Kaufman, and Dennis Carroll. *Subsequent Educational Attainment of High School Dropouts*. Washington, D.C.: U.S. Department of Education, National Center for Education Statistics, NCES 98-085, 1998.

Columbia University Center on Addiction and Substance Abuse. *No Place to Hide: Substance Abuse in Mid-Size Cities and Rural America*. New York: National Center on Addiction and Subtance Abuse, Columbia University (CASA), 1999.

Delisis, Ellen R. "California Colleges, High Schools Collaborate." *Education World*. www.education-world.com, March 2002.

Ericson, Nels. *Addressing the Problem of Juvenile Bullying*. Washington, D.C.: Office of Justice Programs, U.S. Justice Department fact sheet, June 2001.

Goleman, Daniel. *Emotional Intelligence.* New York: Bantam Books, 1995.

Hoover, J.H. "Bullying: Perceptions of Adolescent Victims in Midwestern U.S.A." *School Psychology International.* 1992.

Johnston, Lloyd D. "Table 1: Trends in Lifetime Prevalence of Use of Various Drugs for 8th, 9th, 10th, 12th Graders." *Monitoring the Future Study 2001.* Ann Arbor: University of Michigan, Institute for Social Research, 1991–2001.

Kaiser Family Foundation Survey. *Talking with Kids about Tough Issues.* Washington, D.C. www.cdc.gov, March 8, 2001.

Miller, Amanda. *Violence in U.S. Public Schools: 2000 School Survey on Crime and Safety.* Washington, D.C.: National Center for Education Statistics, www.nces.ed.gov, October 22, 2003.

The National Center for Chronic Disease Prevention and Health Promotion. *Youth Risk Behavior Surveillance System.* Annual survey, June 2002.

The National Institute of Child Health and Human Development. *Health Behavior of School-Aged Children.* School Crime Supplement to the National Crime Victimization Survey. NCVS U.S. Justice Department, 2001.

Rohrman, D. *Combating Truancy in Our Schools, A Community Effort.* NASSP (National Association of Secondary School Principals) Bulletin 76(549) 1993: 40–51.

Romley, Richard. "Truancy a Serious, Costly Problem." *The Prosecutor.* Maricopa County, CA: District Attorney's Office. www.maricopacountyattorney.org, 1998.

Slobogin, Kathy. "Educators Ponder Big Change: Smaller Schools." CNN.com, April 19, 2001.

Surgeon General's Report, U.S. Department of Public Health Service. *Mental Health: A Report of the Surgeon General.* Chap. 3, "Children and Mental Health." Washington, D.C.: U.S. Department of Public Health Service, www.surgeongeneral.gov, 2000.

U.S. Census Bureau. *Households and Families.* Census Brief, September 2001.

U.S. Department of Education. *Subsequent Educational Attainment of High School Dropouts.* Washington, D.C.: National Center for Education Statistics, 1998.

## CHAPTER 2

Cushman, Kathleen. "What Rural Schools Can Teach Urban Systems." *Journal of the Annenberg Challenge.* Providence, RI: Brown University, 1997.

Miller, Amanda. *Violence in U.S. Public Schools: 2000 School Survey on Crime and Safety.* Washington, D.C.: National Center for Education Statistics, www.nces.ed.gov, October 22, 2003.

Peabody, Zanto A. "New Designs Turning Schools into Fortresses." *Los Angeles Times.* June 2, 2001.

Tanner, C. Kenneth. *Essential Aspects of Designing a School.* Athens: The School Design and Planning Laboratory, University of Georgia. www.coe.uga.edu/sdpl.html, April 2000.

Ulloa, Melinda. *Smaller Is Better, New Grants to Help Personalize America's High Schools.* Washington, D.C.: U.S. Department of Education, 2001.

## CHAPTER 3

Goleman, Daniel. *Emotional Intelligence.* New York: Bantam Books, 1995.

## CHAPTER 4

Armstrong, Thomas. *7 Kinds of Smart.* New York: Penguin/Plume, 1993.

Delaney, Bill. "Critics Fear State Test Taking Will Take Its Toll." CNN.com. May 25, 2001.

Gardner, Howard. *The Disciplined Mind: What All Students Should Understand.* New York: Simon and Schuster, 1999.

Gardner, Howard. *Notes on Multiple Intelligences.* Boston, MA: Harvard University Press, 1980.

Goleman, Daniel. *Emotional Intelligence.* New York: Bantam Books, 1995.

Hill, P.T., J.W. Guthrie, and L.C. Pierce. *Reinventing Public Education: How Contracting Can Transform American Schools.* Chicago: University of Chicago Press, 1997.

Pellulo, Willis Mariaemma, and Victoria Hodson. *A Self-Portrait: A Guide to Learning/Working/Communication Styles.* Ventura, CA: Reflective Education Perspectives, 1991.

## CHAPTER 5

Borsuk, Alan J. "Standardized Assessment Is Changing Education." *The Milwaukee Journal Sentinel Online.* June 16, 2001.

Coeyman, Marjorie. "America's Widening Teacher Gap." *Christian Science Monitor.* July 17, 2001.

Flora, Charles. "Teacher Hopes to Ignite Spark in Uninvolved Students." *Ventura County Star.* April 19, 1998.

Gerald, Debra E., and William Hussar. *Projections of Education Statistics to 2012.* Washington, D.C.: National Center for Education Statistics. www.nces.ed.gov//pubs2002/proj2012/, 2001.

Hill, P.T., J.W. Guthrie, and L.C. Pierce. *Reinventing Public Education: How Contracting Can Transform American Schools.* Chicago: University of Chicago Press, 1997.

Horatio Alger Association. *State of Our Nation's Youth.* www.horatioalger.com, 2001.

Ingersoll, Richard M. "Teacher Turnover, Teacher Shortages, and the Organization of Schools." *Policy Brief #3*, Center for the Study of Teaching and Policy. Seattle: University of Washington, January 2001.

Krishnamurti, Jiddu. *Education and the Significance of Life.* San Francisco, CA: HarperSan Francisco, 1981.

Madrigal, Jeff. "Teacher's Lament." *Ojai Valley News.* April 6, 2001.

The National Teacher Recruitment Clearing House. *The Urban Challenge: Teacher Demand and Supply in the Great City Schools.* Belmont, MA: Recruiting New Teachers, www.rnt.org, 2003.

O'Donohue, John. *Anam Cara, A Book of Celtic Wisdom.* New York: Harper-Collins, 1997.

Smith, Lawrence L. "Technology in Teaching." *USA Today Magazine.* March 1999.

U.S. Census Bureau. *Back to School.* Washington, D.C.: U.S. Census Bureau Public Information Office, February 11, 2003.

Wigginton, Eliot. *Sometimes a Shining Moment: The Foxfire Experience—Twenty Years Teaching in a High School Classroom.* New York: Anchor/ Doubleday, 1986.

## CHAPTER 6

Colvin, Richard Lee, and Duke Helfand. "Special Education a Failure on Many Fronts." *Los Angeles Times.* www.latimes.com, April 9, 2001.

McCombs, Kathryn, and Dennis Moore. *Substance Abuse Prevention and Intervention for Students with Disabilities: A Call to Educators.* Arlington, VA: ERIC Clearinghouse on Disabilities and Gifted Education, ERIC EC Digest #E627, August 2002.

National Institute of Child Health and Development. *Why Children Succeed or Fail at Reading.* Washington, D.C., 2001.

National Institute of Mental Health. *Learning Disabilities.* Washington, D.C., NIH Publication No. 93-3611, 1993.

U.S. Department of Education. *A Disproportionate Share of Students with Disabilities Dropped Out of School.* Washington, D.C.: Office of Special Education Programs, National Longitudinal Transition Study, 1993.

U.S. Department of Education. *Increase in Learning Disabled Students Attending U.S. Public Schools between 1990 and 1999.* Washington, D.C.: Office of Special Education Programs, Data Analysis System, 2001.

U.S. Department of Education. *Number of Students Ages 6 through 21 Served Under IDEA.* Washington, D.C.: Office of Special Education Programs, Data Analysis System Table II-2, 2000.

Weaver, Diane. "Statistics Confirm Rise in Childhood ADHD and Medication Use." *Education World*. www.education-world.com, December 2000.

## CHAPTER 7

Carnegie Council on Adolescent Development. *Turning Points: for the 21st Century. Preparing American Youth*. New York, www.carnegie.org, 1989.

## CHAPTER 8

Carroll, Rebecca. "Back to School: More Families Opting to Home School Their Children." Home School Legal Defense Assn. www.hslda.org, August 24, 2003.

Coeyman, Marjorie. "Social Entrepreneurs Eagerly Move Forward." *Christian Science Monitor*. April 27, 1999.

Hammond, Bill. "Ask an Expert: What Is Philosophy of Alternative Education?" CNN.com, November 29, 2000.

Mancuso, Anthony. "How to Form a Nonprofit Corporation." *Non-Profit Corporation Handbook*. Berkeley, CA: Nolo Press, 2002.

Smith, Hedrick. "Why These Schools Work." *Parade Magazine*. January 4, 1998, p. 12.

# Index

## About the Authors

ELLEN HALL is director of Oak Grove School, an alternative pre-K–12 school in Ojai, CA.

RICHARD HANDLEY is a features reporter for the *Ventura County Reporter* and Director, Environmental Education Programs, Ojai Valley Land Conservancy.